COUNTRYMAN'S
COOKING

* ❀ * ❀ * ❀ * ❀ * ❀ * ❀ * ❀ * ❀ * ❀ * ❀ * ❀ *

COUNTRYMAN'S
COOKING

* ❀ * ❀ * ❀ * ❀ * ❀ * ❀ * ❀ * ❀ * ❀ * ❀ * ❀ *

W. M. W. Fowler

EXCELLENT PRESS
LUDLOW

First published in 1965
This edition published in 2006 by
Excellent Press
9 Lower Raven Lane
Ludlow
Shropshire
SY8 1BW

A copy of the British Library Cataloguing in Publication Data
for this title is available from the British Library

ISBN 1 900318 29 6

Printed and bound in Great Britain by
TJ International Ltd

To Slosh,
whose idea it was,
and all those other people who,
by their kindness, knowledge
and patience, have taught me
much of the material in this book.
Not forgetting the Flossies
and Letties of this world—
without whom it would indeed
be a dull place.

CONTENTS

Introduction

INTRODUCTION

THIS book is written for men. Men who, through choice or circumstance, live on their own, so that they can give a small dinner party and at the same time remain on speaking terms with their friends.

As a small boy I was brought up, during term time, in a household where the strange late-Victorian theory prevailed that it was *infra dig* for the girls of the family to concern themselves with such mundane matters as the selection, preparation and cooking of food. Instead, my mother and my aunts had all been trained in the Arts—Painting, Music, Woodcarving, Languages, etc. And very good they were at it, too—but oh dear! Those meals! I can remember them to this day. The staff consisted of two young girls, usually from one of the Northumbrian mining villages, who had just left school. Nice, cheerful youngsters most of them were, who used to find time to play "Cowboys and Indians" with me sometimes—time stolen from their Herculean task of keeping that great five-storey terraced barracks of a house in some sort of order. Their cooking (bless them!) consisted of The Stew and The Roast. Stew being an unidentifiable lump of meat, hacked into bits—fat, gristle and all—combined with similarly treated vegetables, and boiled till a watery soup with bits of leather and rubber bobbing about in it was achieved. The Roast, on the other hand, was simpler. On Sunday morning the fire in the great black range in the cavernous kitchen was stoked up till it roared; the dampers were pulled out and The Joint, in a big square tin, was Committed to the Flames. This was literally true on at least one occasion—the magic morning when the oven caught fire. One of the girls opened the door to see how things were doing, to be greeted by a sheet of flame. Wisely shutting the door again, she reported to my uncle, a tall, dour, pale-eyed Scots engineer. Muttering "silly women" he descended to the kitchen "to put a stop to this nonsense" and lost his eyebrows in the ensuing blast. I remember decamping hurriedly so that I could "fall about" without fear of retribution.

Then came Public School Food. All P.S.F. was rough, but some was rougher than others. Mine must have been among the roughest. Whether the same system applies today I do not know, but at that time a house-master was given a lump sum at the beginning of each term on which to feed his House. What he could save out of this money he was allowed to put in his own pocket. Some House-masters were honest, humane men; others weren't.

Army cookery, and, at the beginning of the War, Air Force, followed on. In those days all the squadron officers were allotted a job besides their flying, and mine at one station was Airmen's Mess. There had been a lot of complaints from the men about their food—which I found amply justified when I started investigating. The rations, when they came in, were good, but by the time the cooks had finished with them they weren't worth eating. Where the fault lay was obvious even to a very young Pilot Officer. I earned the undying hatred of the Sergeant Cook—who was a knave as well as a fool—but the grub gradually improved until, in the end, it was quite eatable. I acquired a rudimentary knowledge of cooking from this experience and also an interest in it. A long spell as a Prisoner of War—when food was literally more valuable than gold—heightened the interest but gave little scope for much practice, except the stewing of the Kommandant's cat with one black market onion! Conversation only turns to food when there isn't any; and men from all over the world made each other's mouths water with descriptions of wonderful dishes from their home countries, and minute details as to how they were made. People wrote these receipts down in little books and "collected" them! (No one can dig tunnels all the time!) I remember one Malayan dish of about ten ingredients had only two that I had ever heard of.

Then, at last, the War ended and I came home to live, mostly on my own, in a cottage in one of the wildest parts of

England. Rationing was, of course, still on and a large proportion of my diet was provided by my gun and fishing rod.
The preparation of game, plucking, drawing, skinning, etc.
didn't present any problem as this was always a chore I got
saddled with as a lad, but plain boiled curlew and rabbit,
even when embellished with a handful or two of dried peas,
becomes rather tedious after a time. There are few things nicer
than fried trout and bacon, but at the same time I began to
think "There must be some other way!"

And so, many years later, and after many experiments, a
simple and (so people say) effective pattern of cooking took
shape.

Finally, I would like to make it quite clear that the instructions I shall give are my personal opinions only. There may be,
and probably are, equally effective ways of achieving the same
object, so I will not continually excuse myself with "In my
opinions" and "I personally thinks".

EQUIPMENT

There is nothing esoteric or mysterious about the preparation
and cooking of food. The process can be divided into two main
parts and a set of efficient gear is needed for each half.

The list which I will give is an average one and there is
nothing on it which will remain unused for very long. As far as
possible I will deal with the items of equipment in the order in
which they are likely to be used when some game or meat is
brought into the house.

MEAT HOOKS

Game and joints must always be hung up in as cool and airy
a place as possible. Never lay them on a plate or a slab, or they
will deteriorate much faster. Half a dozen butchers' hooks—
stainless steel preferably—should be enough.

KNIVES

A blunt knife in a kitchen can be put in the same category
as a motor car that won't start, time-wasting and infuriating.
The car usually sees one off with a ricked back and sprained
thumb, the blunt knife, a badly gashed left hand!

The fancy stainless steel efforts sold for the benefit of the kitchen-proud housewife are, to my mind, rubbish. The kind of knife to buy is the one used by the professionals in the particular job you want to do. I would suggest the following collection:

For *Meat:* One 10-inch *Butcher's knife.* Steel, not stainless. One *Slaughterman's skinning knife.* For *vegetables:* One *Chef's chopping knife.* This is a fearsome-looking weapon with a triangular 14-inch blade. The French ones are very good and not as expensive as the German. Its use is not as bloodthirsty as its looks would have you believe, as it is almost entirely for the fine chopping of all kinds of vegetables. The knife is held and, with the elbow as a fixed point, a rapid chopping motion produced—the blade not rising more than about an inch from the board. Meanwhile, with the left hand, the substance to be cut is fed slowly under the edge. The tips of the fingers are kept tucked underneath, and the knuckles are against the side of the blade. Mind you don't forget about your thumb! Time spent watching an expert is not wasted.

Two or three *Victorian table knives.* The ones with real ivory handles are inclined to have blades made of better steel than the others. They may be bought for a bob or two at a junk shop and, when sharpened up are invaluable for a hundred-and-one jobs.

I have found the best way of sharpening kitchen knives is to use a mill file. This is the 8 or 10-inch flat file used for sharpening a circular saw. With a few careful strokes it will cut the required bevel on each side of your blade. Follow this by honing with a slip of very fine carborundum stone, dipped in water. Finally, you will need a *Butcher's "steel"* (a long one with a guard) to keep your knife edge "set up" whilst you are working. For some strange reason the steels provided in "carving sets" have no guard. Therefore, the knife must be sharpened "away from you"—which is not as effective. A butcher's steel has a brass disc just above the handle to protect your hand and, in this case, the blade is drawn down the steel "towards you". Your butcher would be only too pleased to give you a demonstration, I expect.

A pair of *poultry shears* is very useful on occasions, but I have found "tin-snips" equally effective.

A *meat-saw* is also handy, but not essential. The omission of a cleaver (even a small one) from the list is intentional, as you might be tempted to dismember a hare or rabbit with it, instead of jointing it properly, thereby ruining your dish with innumerable chips of bone.

ASSORTED CULINARY TOOLS

A *palette knife* (or spatula). Buy a good one as you will be using it a lot. Blade about 12 inches long by 2 inches wide and made of spring steel; wooden handle.

Two of those large wooden-handled *cooking spoons;* one with slots in it, one without.

Soup ladle and half a dozen *old table spoons* and *forks,* all of which are best bought at the junk shop!

A Pyrex *pipette baster.* This is an excellent gadget.

Large round-bottomed *strainer.*

A thick wooden *chopping board.*

Six assorted *meat dishes* (junk shop again!).

Two large *mixing-bowls*—preferably glass.

POTS & PANS

I will tell you a story and then you can decide for yourself what kind of hollow-ware to buy.

Once upon a time there was a District Commissioner in Darkest Africa. He, like the prince in the fairy story, was as intelligent as he was handsome. So much so that when he returned at the end of his tour of duty, he was knighted and, later, given the Lord Lieutenancy of his county; which, if it does nothing else, shows he was no mug. Whilst investigating disease in his District, he noticed that the first occurrence of cancer among the blacks coincided with their acquisition of aluminium cooking pots. So convinced did he become that his theory was right and aluminium pots were at least a contributory cause of cancer that, when he returned home at the end of his tour, he went into his kitchens and ordered every aluminium cooking vessel to be thrown away. Being a gentleman of some substance, he replaced them with heavy copper pans lined with silver plating.

xiv/*Countryman's Cooking*

One would suppose that, were there an answer to the problem as simple as this, modern science would have been on to it like a flash. But I still don't like the pitting in aluminium pans, nor do I like the discolouration which occurs when certain fruit is cooked in them. And so, almost entirely, I use either iron or enamel. Naturally it doesn't matter with frying pans, because fats and oils do not attack the metal.

And so it's up to you.

Saucepans:	One 1-gallon; two 6-pint; one 3-pint; one 2-pint.
One Pressure Cooker:	To be used entirely as a stock-pot. These unfortunately always seem to be made of aluminium. They can often be picked up cheap at the sale-rooms because their former owners were frightened of them!
One Deep Frying Pan:	With basket.
Frying Pans:	One 12-inch and one 10-inch—heavy aluminium.
Roasting Tins:	Enamel. One Turkey size and one Chicken size.
Casseroles:	Two large, with lids.

PART ONE

The Pheasant
Grouse and Partridge
Pigeons, Waders & Rook
Poultry & Wildfowl

* ✸ *

CHAPTER I

THE PHEASANT

FEW, I think, will argue with me if I say that the pheasant, besides being the most magnificent of British game birds to look at, is also the best to eat.

The origin of the pheasant in this country is rather obscure. Some authorities say it is indigenous, others that it was introduced by the Romans, but the generally accepted theory is that the species known as the Old English Blackneck came from Western Transcaucasia in the misty horizons of Time. Since then it has been crossed with most Asiatic varieties between Caucasia and Japan. The Mongolian is the one with a clear white ring around its neck; the Chinese, probably the largest and most delicately coloured of them all, is much paler than the rest. Melanistic and albino strains are also bred. Ornamental pheasants—Golden, Silver, Reeves, Argus, Amherst, etc.—are aviary birds, and of little importance to either the game preserver or the cook. Although remarkable-looking birds with brilliant plumage, most of the cocks are so aggressive and quarrelsome that they are more trouble in the coverts than they are worth.

The pheasant is mainly a marsh or swamp bird, living in woods and rush-beds near water. He swims quite well, too. The diet is as varied as it well could be—corn, acorns, nuts, berries and fruit of all kinds, bulbs (I remember one of my aunts hopping with rage when she found the pheasants had dug up and eaten all her new, expensive tulip bulbs!), grass and weed seeds, worms, slugs and snails, lizards and adders (cock pheasants have quite a reputation as snake-killers) and occasionally mice—which sometimes choke them.

The hens are, unfortunately, very poor mothers: if she ends up with three chicks reared out of fifteen or sixteen, she is doing well! She can't count, and seems to lose them here and there. They get lost in the long grass and either die of cold and hunger or get snapped up by rats, stoats or cats. Carrion crows are one of their main enemies; not only do they eat the chicks whenever a chance presents itself, but they will clean up a nest of eggs before you can say Jack Robinson.

Considering how stupid pheasants are when they are young, it is surprising how seemingly intelligent and cunning an old cock is. This old stager will do as much damage to a stock as a fox. He is a very large and powerful bird, with spurs like packing needles; and, by driving off any young cock who comes around looking for a mate, he collects himself a harem—probably upwards of half a dozen hens. They all make nests and fill them with eggs—but the trouble is that none of the eggs hatch out because the old fool is sterile. So you've lost at least a couple of dozen birds for next year.

A story to illustrate how difficult it is to shoot all the old cocks off. In the days before the war, when game was preserved more extensively and shooting-parties more formal, an old cock pheasant lived in the gardens of a stately home in this area. He strutted on the lawns in the morning, ignored the dogs, and generally behaved as if he owned the place—until he saw preparations for a shoot being made. Keepers, dogs out of kennels, game-bags, guns, motor cars, the Squire wearing his funny hat. And then he used to fly up on to the roof of the mansion and sit among the chimney-pots till the party returned in the evening, when he flew down again to take command of the gardens. The family used to watch for this caper on shooting days. He finally died of old age—and deserved to!

We will assume that it is October and you have either shot or been given a pheasant (or better still, a brace.) Straight away cut a piece of string about 18″ long, tie the ends together and making a noose by putting the knot through the loop, put it round the bird's neck and hang it up in as cool and airy a place as you can find. A great danger early in the season is bluebottles. Only one blowfly needs to get at your pheasant, undetected, and you have "had it". One way of getting round this is to make a fly-proof cage by using two hoops of wire about 18″ diameter as spreaders for a muslin "sausage", enough being left at the top to tie tightly round the string the bird hangs on. The time a bird should hang depends on many things; temperature, whether cleanly shot or blown half to bits, age, and of course the personal tastes of whoever is going to eat it. So examine the bird for damage. If it has both legs broken and a wing flapping, you can decide to eat it in three days. If, on the other hand, it does not look as if it had been through the blitz, you can hang it for 10 days—the weather being normal for the time of year. Many pheasants are ruined for hanging by the mauling they get from the iron-mouthed crunching brutes that often masquerade as "gun-dogs". There are few sights funnier than the undignified race between a "gnasher" and his owner to get to a fallen bird first!

Examine the spurs: if they are small and rounded at the end, you can be fairly confident of having a young bird; if, on the other hand, they are long horny spikes, you've got an old warrior. Old hens can be picked out by their more robust build and also by the look of the feet. Anyway, it would be a good thing if the Irish law that hen-pheasants must never be shot at any time of the year applied to this country as well. They have quite enough enemies as it is, without adding Man to the list. Having hung the bird long enough, you must now "dress" it. Take it down to the wood-shed (if you pluck it in the kitchen the whole place will be smothered in minute bits of down) sit on a box with a cardboard carton between your knees to pluck into, and start off. A pheasant is the most tedious of all birds to pluck—especially a young hen—because the skin tears so easily, particularly round the neck.

Holding the bird in the left hand, with the head away from you, begin at the back of the neck about three inches above the shoulders and pull the feathers out one at a time, away from you and with a quick tweak. Work round the neck, and when this "danger point" is passed, you will get on more quickly. Pluck the wings as far as the second joint—the wrist—and then clip them off with the tin-snips at that joint. Now draw the sinews in the legs. With a sharp knife, cut the scaly skin round each leg about threequarters of an inch below the "heel", taking care not to cut too deep and sever the tendons, too. Then snap the bone under the cut—a quick pressure with this point against the sharp edge of a table will do it. Now, holding the joint in one hand and the foot in the other—pull! The tendons will draw through the joint and come out clean. If you try and do the same thing from higher up at the joint itself you will find that the sinews will bring half the thigh out with them. If it's an old bird and too strong for you, jamb the foot in the hinge of the door and get both hands on the leg!

Take the head off by cutting the skin round just below the feathers and drawing this back till you can see the point where the neck joins the body. Clip it out here with the tin-snips. Draw the neck out of the skin to the base of the skull, and clip off and keep for making gravy. Now for the crop; this, as you can see, is a bag made of thin membrane situated at the base of the throat. At this time of year it will probably be filled with blackberries, crab-apple, corn and weed seeds, with perhaps an early acorn or two. Work the crop out with the fingers, separating it gently from the skin on one side and the meat on the other. Try not to break it and you will save yourself the trouble of clearing up the resulting mess!

To draw the bird, make a longitudinal cut from just below the breast bone to the vent. Insert the first and second fingers of the right hand and hook out the inside. Cut the heart, gizzard (the large hard flattened sphere) and the liver clear of the rest and put them with the neck. With a knife, cut the vent away completely. Now clean the gizzard by holding it in the left hand, cutting carefully round the edge for about two-thirds of its circumference. If you cut too deep your knife will get into the little stones and quartz that the pheasant has in its crop to grind its food (a bird has no teeth) and will be blunted. Open it out and wash thoroughly, then peel off the leathery lining, or as much of it as you can. Taking the bird in one hand and your plate of giblets in the other, return to the kitchen. Turn on a gas ring and singe the bird over it to remove all the hair-like feathers that remain. If no gas, then a piece of newspaper rolled into a large spill will do—only the smell will be even worse!

To truss the bird, provide yourself with a skewer about 6″

long and some narrow tape or fine string. Now work a leg back under the skin until the knee joint comes opposite the elbow joint on the wing. Insert the skewer through the angles of these two joints at right angles to the fore and aft axis of the bird, and halfway through the carcase. Work the other leg back to be symmetrical with the first and push the skewer on through till it appears behind the knee. Bring the other wing into position and skewer it, too. Tie a piece of string round in front of the skewer to hold the free ends of the wings firmly to the body. Now take another bit of string some 12″ long and tie it in the middle round the "Pope's Nose", with the knot underneath. Bring the ends up, round the legs, above the heel joint, cross over and tie under the "Pope's Nose" again so that when the string is pulled tight the two legs and the P.N. are drawn close together. Reef knot and cut off ends. Cover the whole top of the bird with fat bacon. It is now ready for the oven. A pheasant is not usually stuffed, but some people fill the inside with half-boiled, peeled chestnuts. The object of making the carcase into a compact "ball" is so that it will all cook evenly together, it will remain moist, and no bits will stick out to get burnt.

ROASTING

Again you will find a great variation in instructions. Some will tell you to roast a pheasant for only three-quarters of an hour, this irrespective of age or length of "hang". Start off with your oven "hot"—by which I do not mean red-hot, which would burn the fat and juices which will run out of the bird as it cooks and will be used to flavour the gravy.

Preferably place the bird on a trivet, or rack, in your smaller roasting tin. Put the lid on, and place in the oven. Keep the heat high till you can hear that happy crackling, bubbling, sizzling noise, accompanied by a very pleasant smell.—NOT a menacing roar and a cloud of blue smoke when you open the oven door! Then cut the heat down till the sound remains the same and the smell grows even pleasanter. I will not attempt to give the actual temperatures in degrees F. or C. because I have never owned an oven thermometer—and you probably haven't one either.

Before you started to truss the pheasant you ought to have washed the giblets and put them in a saucepan with a pint of water and a little salt and left them simmering by the fire.

One of the reasons that Roast Pheasant is one of the finest dinners you can offer anyone is that the "trimmings" that go with it are so good. Whilst the roasting is going on you get on with making these.

BREAD SAUCE

In about threequarters of a pint of milk put three bay leaves, a dozen black peppercorns, 4 cloves, a sliced-up small onion and a little salt. Bring to the boil and simmer for half an hour. Cut six slices of white bread, $\frac{1}{4}''$ thick, and cut off the crusts. Cut again both ways, so that you have a heap of little squares of soft bread. Put a handful into a suitably sized bowl and pour on some of the seasoned milk, through a strainer. Keep adding more bread and more milk, stirring the while and retaining the consistency you require. Finally, add a lump of butter and stir till all the lumpiness has smoothed out. Keep warm in the oven.

FRIED CRUMBS

Crush up some oven-dried bread, either by putting it through the mincer or with a rolling pin. Fry in butter (surprising how much butter it takes). Season with a little Cayenne pepper—just a pinch. You must keep turning with a spatula all the time it is cooking. Take it out as soon as the colour starts darkening.

BACON ROLLS

Smoked flitch is probably the best for this purpose. Take the rind off, cut in half, and make each half into a roll with a half-inch hole in the middle. Put the rolls on a skewer.

After the pheasant has been roasting for an hour, take it out of the oven (remembering to shut the door) and baste it. Replace without the cover and lay the skewer of bacon rolls on top. Cook for another half hour and it should be done. I find the best final test of whether a bird is cooked enough is to pull out the skewer, cut the skin round one of the legs and, holding the bird steady, press the leg outwards and downwards. If it comes down easily and the hip joint dislocates, it is done. If it is still a bit springy, give it a little longer. After the pheasant has been taken out of the oven and put on a dish to keep warm, pour off all but about a tablespoonful of fat out of the roasting dish and scatter a desertspoon of flour in. Mix this thoroughly, and then add the stock you have made from the giblets. Boil and stir till a smooth gravy is made. Test for salt.

The usual vegetables to accompany this meal are game chips, creamed potato, and brussels sprouts. A bottle of Burgundy doesn't come amiss either!

A good idea given to me by an old shooting friend—if you only have one pheasant and more than three people to feed, roast a chicken along with it. The artificially fed and reared modern chicken, having no taste of its own, will take on the pheasant's flavour to quite a remarkable extent.

* ❁ *

GROUSE AND PARTRIDGE

* ❁ *

GROUSE

THE main point here is to be able to distinguish a young from an old bird. The expert poulterer can tell by a glance at the feet, but without his knowledge the safest way is to hold the bird up by the lower mandible, between the finger and thumb, and jiggle up and down. If the mandible bends or breaks the bird is young. Otherwise it probably is not. Pressure on top of the skull with the thumb is another test—if the skull crushes easily it is a young one.

There is nothing wrong with an old grouse, it is excellent in a casserole, but you must not try to roast it. Length of time to hang seems to be a matter of personal preference. On the Twelfth (or whatever the opening date is now) grouse are flown from Scotland to London and New York and served in the hotels that same night. But that does not mean to say they would not have been tenderer and of a better flavour had they been hung a couple of days. *Any* meat ought to be hung for at least two or three days before it is cooked. It is part of the cook's job, just as much as the preparation and actual cooking, to know how long his various meats should hang.

The "maturing" process in meat is, I understand, brought about by various enzymes and bacteria already present. These break down the fibres, making the meat tender and also cause chemical changes which improve the flavour. So you have two main factors to balance together (having made absolutely certain your larder is proof against bluebottles), the age of the animal or bird you are dealing with, and the temperature and type of weather at the time. Thundery weather is well known for making foodstuffs decompose more rapidly. "Ionized particles in the air" the Boffins say!

GROUSE CASSEROLE (*Old birds*)

Hang for five or six days according to the weather, and then pluck and draw as for pheasant; then, using a knife and shears, cut the birds in half, lengthwise.

Now make a marinade (which is the liquid in which meat is steeped prior to certain kinds of cooking). The usual main ingredient is red wine, but I have found dry draught cider to be just as good, in fact better for some things, and considerably cheaper. Into a large bowl put one finely sliced onion, then the grouse, pepper (fresh ground black) and salt and, finally, cover with cheap red wine. Leave to soak overnight.

Remove the grouse from the marinade, dry it, roll it in flour and fry it in olive oil (or a mixture of olive oil and butter, if you prefer) and put it in a casserole of the right size—that is, one which will need as little liquid as possible to cover the contents. Pour on the marinade and add a clove of chopped garlic, if you like it, a quarter pound of mushrooms, a pinch of Cayenne pepper and a sprinkling of thyme. Add water to cover if necessary. Bring to the boil in the oven and simmer for as long as required for the meat to lift easily off the bone. Probably about one-and-a-half hours. In August and September the choice of vegetables is almost unlimited, but scarlet runner beans and creamed potatoes would seem to go well with this dish.

PARTRIDGE

The preparation and cooking of partridge is similar to pheasant and grouse. If it is a young bird it is at its best when roasted. If an old one, casserole it.

Apart from its use as an "ordinary" dish, cold roast grouse or partridge, with hot fried bacon and fried bread, makes an exceedingly good breakfast.

There are, of course, many complicated recipes for cooking game—different sauces, different garnishes, etc., but as this book sets out to instruct in first principles and basic techniques I will leave you to turn to Escoffier, or some other master, for the refinements.

* ✿ *

CHAPTER III

PIGEONS, WADERS & ROOK

STANDING in front of a roaring log fire on an autumn evening, my stomach stuck out and my thumbs hooked into the armholes of my weskit, if I wore one, I have no hesitation in proclaiming pompously that Woodpigeon, shot on the corn-fields and stubbles in September and October, and properly casseroled in beer, makes a dish fit for a king. Mellowed by this very meal, washed down with a bottle of claret, I will go even further; there is no better bird that you can use in a casserole.

Whether it is just the perversity of human nature, or a kind of unconscious snobbery, I never understand; but it is fact that when an item of food is plentiful and cheap—the cheapness appears to be the key—people will despise it and buy something twice as expensive and half as good. Rabbits, herring, pigeons and rooks are typical examples. As usual, it is the people who can least afford it who are most guilty of this particular form of daftness. If it were possible, by a clever propaganda campaign, to convince people that pigeon is a delicacy—which it is—instead of classing it as vermin which, with the exception of the hordes of Continental birds that ravage the green-crops in winter, it is not, the Pigeon Problem would largely solve itself. As things stand at present, a poulterer will pay sixpence a pigeon—that is if he will take them at all. This, with cartridges at around 15/6d. for a box of 25, is hardly an encouraging proposition, even for Dead-eye Dick! If, on the other hand, the Populace, especially the Townspeople—who would provide the largest market—were taught, not only how good pigeon pie is, but also how easy pigeons are to prepare and cook, then the poulterer would be able to pay 2/- to 2/6d. a bird, reselling at about a bob profit. Result: more sport, more pigeon-pie and less pigeons. (Why doesn't a deputation turn up and implore me, on bended knees, to be Minister of Agriculture?)

I will suppose that you have been out since mid-day, sitting in your hide built in the hedge out of corn-sheaves or brush-wood, shooting the pigeons as they come swinging in to feed—setting up those already shot, a forked stick to keep their heads up and heading into wind, as decoys to bring others within range. You come home, pretty pleased with yourself, having shot half a dozen—and missed another ten! Take them out of the boot of your car as soon as possible and, coupling them together in pairs, couples or braces, hang them up in a cool airy larder.

Assuming that it is September, the pigeons will only need hanging for two to three days. Take great care that no blue-bottles have been able to get at them, either in the car or the larder. Pigeon is a very easy bird to pluck, the feathers being loose and the skin tough. In fact, the feathers come out so easily that many dogs will dodge retrieving them if they get a chance. A year or so ago, when I was shooting pigeon coming in to the patches of bilberries on the fell, I had a young Springer dog with me. A pigeon fell among the heather about thirty yards out and I sent Joe down from the crag, where the hide was, to bring it in. He found it and brought it a few yards, then dropped it and came trotting back with a feather stuck on the end of his nose. I sent him out again, having lectured him on the errors of his ways. This time he fetched it to the foot of the crag, put it gently down, looked up at me rather sourly, blew a cloud of feathers out of his mouth, climbed slowly up again and sat down beside me. Threats and cajolery were of no avail—I fetched that one myself. I think it must have been a very young bird because the feathers literally fell out of it. They aren't all as bad as that.

The reason that I have put pigeons, waders and rooks all in the same chapter is that the method of dressing and cook-ing is the same, basically for the lot. Dressing is done as follows:

Lay the bird on its back with the head away from you and then, using the thumbs, part the feathers covering the breast-bone. With a sharp knife, slit the skin down the top of the bone. Using the thumbs again, work the skin back and down, leaving the meat of the breast exposed. Continue down the shoulders where, incidentally, you will find the skin sticks tight to the meat right on the point—a nick with your knife will clear this—and skin out half the upper arm. With tin-snips or shears, cut this bone through. Now, with the knife, cut a lateral slit under the point of the breast-bone; put your left thumb through this hole and hold the bird firmly to the table; hook your right thumb under the point of the breast-bone and pull up and away from you—rather as if you were opening a box—and finally, getting a good grip with both hands, give a strong tug upwards, tearing the breast completely away from the rest of the carcase. Pick the adhering feathers off, and you will find that you have almost all the edible part of the bird in one neat lump, stuck handily on to a wafer-thin bone to keep it in shape. You can, if you like, take the legs off too; but I have found that this is not really worth the trouble. There is very little on them. The only other piece worth taking is the liver. Remove this before throwing the remarkably light remains in the junk bucket. The reason for this method of dressing is not, as might be supposed, entirely idleness. The backbone of a pigeon, in common with the pelvis of a rabbit, spoils the flavour of your dish if it is put in. It produces a strange bitter taste as a rule. If you want to have roast pigeon, you must choose only the young ones. Again, description without demonstration is difficult, but you can tell the young ones by their smaller size and rather scruffy appearance compared with the adult. The beak looks too large for the head, and they have not yet grown the white ring around the neck. The feet and legs are, as a rule, not such a bright coral colour as in the full-grown bird.

The plucking, drawing and trussing are the same as for any other bird, but easier than most. I leave the feet on (a) because it is less trouble than taking them off, and (b) because it simplifies tying the legs together when trussing. The roasting is pretty straightforward, but, as pigeon is liable to be rather dry, it is a good thing to put more fat bacon than usual over the top, and to roast in a covered tin—slowly. In point of fact, this is not roasting at all—it is a cross between baking and steaming. True roasting consists of hanging a lump of meat in front of a large fire in such a position that it is out of the smoke, and far enough from the heat not to burn, allowing for the fact that it is being slowly turned all the time on a spit or jack, worked by scullion, dog, or clockwork motor. It is then cooked by the direct heat from the flames—radiation. What we call roasting these days, in an oven, is actually cooking by convection, or hot air. Which is baking, really. The only two forms of true roasting that still survive today are barbequeing (or cooking on a spit over a bed of glowing charcoal) and grilling, where the food is laid on a rack and cooked by means of an electric element brought down from above.

I wonder how, and when, the old wives' tale originated that, if you eat pigeon every day for a week, it will kill you? I suspect that some mediæval wench, getting sick of plucking and cooking pigeons for her gutsy spouse, thought it up—with typical low feminine cunning—to divert him back on to wild boar pie, which she could buy without any trouble from Ye Olde Pie Shoppe, next door to Merrie John, Ye Cobbler, who was a chum of hers anyway—thereby killing Two Birdies with One Stonie!

To return, then, to the pigeon breasts which you have prepared. In passing, notice the size of the breast (which, of course is the wing muscles of the bird) compared with the legs; and then think of the proportions of a cock chicken. The Airborne and the Earthbound.

Put the pieces and the liver in a marinade of draught beer, with added sliced, raw onion, salt, pepper, and such herbs as you prefer. I like bay-leaves. Leave to soak overnight. The kind of beer you use is up to you. Experiment and see whether you prefer mild, bitter or old ale; but don't use bottled beer if you can possibly help it, the effect is not the same. Red wine is also very nice for this purpose, but I have found it rather wasteful and prefer to cook in beer, keeping the wine to drink with the meal.

Take the meat out of the marinade, dry it, flour it, and fry it in olive oil. Pack the pieces as tightly as possible into a casserole, and pour on the marinade. Top up with beer or water to cover, if necessary. Simmer in the oven for anything from threequarters of an hour to an hour-and-a-half. When the meat can be prised away from the bone without much difficulty, it is cooked. Remove the pigeon to another plate and strain the gravy in to a small saucepan. If it needs reducing, boil it down to the required quantity and, if it needs thickening, stir in a beaten egg yolk after it has come off the boil. Whether or not to put a glass of port in at this stage depends entirely on your own palate. Either you will think that the slight sweetness improves it or spoils it. Pour the gravy back over the pigeon, which has been replaced in the casserole, and put it in the oven till needed. The method of pastry-making, if you want a pigeon pie, is identical with that employed in Rabbit Pie and Beef-steak and Kidney Pie.

Creamed potato is a suitable form to go with this, as there will be quite a lot of gravy. Broad beans, Scarlet runners and Brussel sprouts are especially good as a second vegetable, because they are all served dry. Avoid a vegetable which needs a sauce of its own—such as celery, marrow, etc.—or the meal will become too sloppy.

The foregoing instructions are the same for all the rest of the birds included in this chapter, both dressing and cooking. You will, of course, vary the flavourings to fall in with your own personal likes and dislikes—which is as it should be. I find the so-called gourmets and self-styled epicures extraordinarily irritating. Why should someone be scorned as a lout, or jeered at as an ignoramus, merely because he prefers egg sauce with his salmon, instead of shrimp; or drinks Burgundy with his pheasant instead of a white wine? It's absolute nonsense. If a man likes eating kippers spread with raspberry jam—as, so I am told, is done in parts of North East England—then jolly good luck to him. He doesn't tell me that I also must eat them. It is generally accepted that men's tastes vary enormously in such important subjects as Beer, Women, Sport, Motor-cars, and other pleasures of life. But when it comes to Art, Music, Food and Politics, all kinds of weirdies and crackpots creep out from under their flat stones and do their utmost to cram their worthless opinions down their fellows' throats. Very odd.

WADERS

These are the birds of the tide's edge. All of them, as far as I know, are edible; and a lot are extremely eatable. Roughly, the ones you are likely to come across are:

CURLEW

This is the largest and, in the Autumn, probably the best to eat. But quite apart from this, it is a wonderful bird—unmistakable, with its long curved beak and dappled brown and white plumage, and long green legs. Rather larger than a pigeon, it is very strong on the wing and is one of the few birds that flies at night. Wild, almost eerie—one of the most exciting sounds I know is that of the curlew flocks calling to each other, far up under the stars, on a late February night, as they flight in from the estuary and up into the mountains to choose their nesting sites. Robert Louis Stevenson thought of them when he knew he was to die in a foreign land—"And where the whaups are crying I do remember——". They seem to know they are safe in the breeding season, and often become quite tame—for a curlew! But, come Autumn, when the great flocks gather up on the shores and estuaries, he is a horse of a very different colour. Probably the keenest-sighted of all wildfowl and game-birds put together, it takes good camouflage and complete immobility if his attention is not to be attracted to the crouching gunner. His jink and swerve is masterly—just the thing the war-time bombers needed when a German fighter came in to attack.

PLOVER

Both green and golden are excellent to eat. Although not really waders in the sense that they do not spend their lives paddling around the shore, they are near enough to be included in this section. Green plover are protected under the Wild Birds Protection Act, both birds and eggs. Plovers' eggs were so highly esteemed at one time that the species was being exterminated—hence the regulations—but now there seem to be large flocks of lapwing almost everywhere, so perhaps it will presently be put into the Wildfowl category.

Probably the best way of cooking these birds is to pluck and draw them, put them on a half-inch thick slice of bread spread with butter or bacon fat, lay fat bacon over the top and roast them. In Victorian times, when plover was eaten more than it is now, it was customary to leave the feet on golden plover (which was supposed to be the better) so that the diner could be sure he was getting the right thing. One has more toes than the other. I can never remember which!

OYSTER CATCHER

A very handsome bird, with his black and white plumage and red beak and legs, he looks, you may think, rather too like a seagull. In spite of this you will find that, dressed and casseroled in the same way as pigeon, he will make a good meal.

REDSHANK & GREENSHANK

The only time you are likely to shoot one of these is when, after a long, muddy and arduous stalk towards a flock of duck, the whole operation is ruined by one hysterical, screaming redshank hurling itself out of a creek and warning everything within a quarter of a mile of your presence. They are very small, and hardly worth bothering about.

Other species include Knot, Godwit, Sandpiper, Sanderling, Dunlin, Turnstone and, smallest of all, Stint. With the possible exception of a series of lucky flock-shots, you would never shoot enough of these to make it worth while.

ROOKS

Farmers and gamekeepers all seem to agree that there are too many rooks, and yet nothing much is done about it these days. Judging by the number and quality of the rook-rifles made at the end of the last century and the beginning of this, rook shooting must have been one of the more popular Minor Field Sports. The only organised example I have ever seen was when I was at school in a cathedral city. The leaves would just be coming out on the great beeches and elms along the river banks when a procession of venerable old gentlemen would sally forth from the Cathedral Close, carrying .410 shot guns more as if they were pieces of ecclesiastic regalia than lethal weapons.

The party wound its way, with due solemnity, down the Baily and over the ancient stone bridge above the weir, pausing to watch the rooks—who seemed to know something was cookin'—wheeling and cawing over the tree tops, before ascending to the Heights of Abraham, where the ritual slaughter of the innocents was to take place. About half a dozen of us lads followed respectfully in the rear—self-appointed acolytes, whose duties consisted of rook-spotting for the blood-thirsty clerics and retrieving the victims. Sometimes Christian charity would get the better of the blood-lust, and a gun was handed to one of us with "Have a go at that one, boy." The joy, to a thirteen-year-old, of blasting off a rook with the Archdeacon's own gun would have to be experienced to be appreciated. I can see that little gun now: single barrel, side lever, and with a big dog's head hammer. The 2″ yellow cartridges, and the smell of burnt nitro-powder when the breech was opened. The lines one would get for the algebra one had not done, and the beating that inevitably followed any originality or initiative in those days, were all forgotten in that moment.

As soon as possible after the shooting party had returned, reeking of sanctity and gunpowder, to their cloisters, a chum and I would return to the battlefield, with catapults, to polish off the pricked and wounded birds that were always missed in the "gathering". Although I sez it m'self as shouldn't, I was an exceedingly good shot with a catapult. In fact, at times I was brilliant! The weapon was made according to instructions given to my father when he was a lad, by a keeper's son in the

New Forest. The stock—I have it yet somewhere—of ash, the colour and patina of old ivory. About a foot long and curved like a spoon, the U at the end two-and-a-half inches long and an inch-and-a-half across the horns, carved and sandpapered till its symmetry was perfect. The $\frac{1}{8}''$ square elastic of such length that it was fully extended when the left arm, holding the stock, was right out, and the pouch, holding its SSG shot, was drawn back behind the right ear. The elastic was carefully protected with little sleeves of kid, so that the waxed flax bindings should not cut it.

The target which I used to practice on, hour after hour, was a large round toffee tin, with two or three dusters inside to prevent the buckshot getting distorted, and with a sheet of strong white paper tied over the top, as if it were a drum. The silhouette of a sparrow was then painted in the middle with Indian ink. At ranges of between five and fifteen yards, and at various angles, I shot till the sparrow was no more. I suppose it is a good thing from the point of view of both the Public and the Police that the art of making and using catapults has almost died out. They are more powerful than an air-pistol (having a lower velocity but a far heavier projectile) completely silent, and very easily concealed.

It was on one of these illegal expeditions along the river banks one afternoon that I heard, round the bend of the little path I was on, the voices of a woman and a child, coming my way. I melted into a rhododendron clump and lay low. Presently my *bête noir* and his mother hove in sight. A horrible little boy he was; about six years old, with a bright red nose that always needed blowing, and bright red ears that stuck out from his head like jug-handles. The son of one of the Minor Canons of the Cathedral, the little brat was a natural mischief-maker and sneak. Whenever his beady eyes spotted us climbing trees, sailing our straw bashers down the stream, or otherwise harmlessly diverting ourselves, his revolting treble would pipe up "Look at the naughty boys, Mummy". Mummy, not having the sense she was born with, instead of belting his ear'ole, would as likely as not report us to our house-master. More trouble.

As they came opposite to my rhododendron bush the dear little lad stopped and began examining something in the grass on the far side of the path. His mother walked on. He bent further down, till his corduroy breeches (with pants hanging down underneath) were tight as a drum. The temptation was too much. Range about ten yards. The buckshot smacked home with a most satisfying sound. He shot up in the air with a shriek like a train whistle, both hands clapped to his backside. Mummy came rushing back and took his trousers down to see what had happened to darling Clarence. It was a honey of a shot—I could see the blue spot of the strike bang in the middle of one buttock. How I managed to stop laughing out loud I shall never know. As a variety turn it was terrific. They decided, in the end, that he had been stung by a hornet. To this day I can see the little stinker snivelling off up the path, rubbing his bottom! So perish all traitors!

During this digression, however, the young rooks are still swaying about in the tree tops. It is only the young ones that are fit to eat. There are a few days between the time that they leave the nest, and the time they can fly. During daylight they come out and sit on the branches close by, swaying in the wind. If the season is early and the leaves are out, they are very difficult to spot and one's neck develops a marvellous crick after a few hours of wandering around with nose pointing skyward. These days a .22 rifle firing short solid-nose ammunition is generally used, instead of the central fire .30 rook rifle or a .410 shot gun. The cost of cartridges for both these is prohibitive now.

A point to watch when gathering the slain for your own use: sometimes a carrion crow will nest in a rookery, and on several occasions I have found young crows in the bag. These would, somewhat naturally, considering their diet, not enhance the flavour of the stew. They are easy to weed out. A rook has a stop, or step, between the base of the beak and the forehead. A carrion crow has not. Therefore throw away anything with a Grecian profile.

It was a colonel of Gunners who taught me how to dress rooks. One of the real old sort, he believed in being able to do anything his minions could—and better. "No good leaving this to Tom, m' boy. He'd just make a hash of it." The operation was, I remember, carried out in the coach-house. The old lad sat on a box, with a pile of rooks on one side of him and a huge Victorian willow-pattern meat dish on the other. The *modus operandi*, as they would have said in those days, was exactly as I have described for preparing pigeons for stewing. Half an hour later the dish was full of rook breasts, lined up as if for General Inspection; and the floor was a shambles of blood, guts and feathers. "Tom! TOM! Where's that idle loafing lout got himself to this time?" "Ah, there you are Tom. Be a good chap and clear this mess up for me will you?" "Very good Colonel." And as the old warrior marched off to the house with his dish of rooks—"Marvellous chap, Tom. Used to be m' batman in India. Don't know what I'd do without him."

Rook pie traditionally has steak in it as well. Why this is so I do not know. Perhaps rook was so prized at one time that one seldom got enough of them. Use any kind of beef you like, topside, shoulder or shin; but whichever you do use you must cook it first of all to within about half an hour of its proper time before the rooks are put in. They, being so young, will cook very quickly, so you must do a bit of handicapping. Flour and fry in the usual manner, and include what cooking liquor and flavourings you have found you like best. For pie-crust instructions, see Rabbit Pie and Beefsteak and Kidney Pie.

* ✤ *

CHAPTER IV

POULTRY & WILDFOWL

A MAN must indeed be insensitive if there is no sight or sound that will make the hair up the back of his neck bristle and tears run down his cheeks with sheer emotional excitement. An aircraft flying very low and very fast; a battalion of one of the crack Highland Regiments marching through their home town with fixed bayonets and the pipes playing; one of the famous Glasgow-London expresses coming down off Shap Fell at night, not far short of 100 mph. racing thro' a station in a blaze of light and with an earth-shuddering roar. But the one that gets me more than any other is the sight and sound of the wild geese coming in after their fantastic flight from the Arctic. A faint clamour, like distant hounds, makes me look to the Northern sky and here they come, far above the fell, a wide-spread wavering echelon—five hundred strong. Now I can see the individual birds. Their talking becomes louder and more excited as they sight home—the Duddon Sands and the huge estuary of Morecambe Bay, formed by the Leven, the Kent and the Lune. Thousands of acres of sand-bars where they can rest secure and regain their strength after a nonstop flight of possibly fifteen hundred miles.

As I watch them grow hazy in the distance a renewed calling makes me look up to see a second arrow-head passing over. Each bird out of the slipstream of the one in front of it, the slow beat of their wings carrying them along at a tremendous pace. Sometimes the leaders will change places, a fresh Wing Commander moving in to rest the weary one. It is said that some of the old geese must have done the journey twice a year for over thirty years. Romantic nonsense, you may say, but I can't help feeling that such a gallant, stout-hearted bird deserves better of us when he reaches our shores, than a charge of buck-shot. I cannot resist remarking that this could be reserved, more appropriately, for some of our other visitors!

A wild goose is no easy bird to shoot, except in snow or fog; and to bag one is something of a triumph, but be content with shooting one in your lifetime. It is very unlikely that you will be able to eat it anyway. Many inedible old birds would have to be needlessly massacred for every young eatable one. Therefore, you will find no culinary mention of the wild goose in this book.

GOOSE

I have no such scruples as far as the domestic variety is concerned. An arrogant loafing bird who spends his life bullying the chickens and frightening little girls with bare legs —and little boys too, come to that! I still remember a humdinger of a peck I got as a little lad.

If you possibly can, get your goose ready plucked and dressed. The very worst that can happen to you is to be given a sack with a live goose inside. So we'd better start there. First of all, unless you really want a pet goose, don't open the sack. Otherwise you, or some other mug, will say "Ah! The poor thing. It seems a shame to bump it off," and you'll be lumbered with the great stupid dirty brute plodging round your garden for the next two decades. Take the sack out of the boot of your motor and place it gently on the grass. Go away and find a heavy stick about two feet long and an inch thick, a sharp knife and a piece of string. When you get back you will find that the goose is trying to put its head up, thereby making a bulge in the sack with the top of its skull. Smite this bulge good and hearty, whereupon the goose will lose all interest in future proceedings. Take it out of the sack, cut its throat, and hang it up by the feet with the piece of string to some handy tree branch. By the time it comes round from the belt over the head, it will have bled to death. Which sounds a bit Irish but is nevertheless true. There are some disgraceful and barbarous methods of killing geese but I think the foregoing is as humane as it well could be.

The bulge in the sack reminds me of a very regrettable incident that happened when the 1st Battalion of my Regiment had a C.S.M. with all the bad qualities of the old-fashioned

N.C.O. and none of his many virtues. In fact, the fellow was agreed by all ranks to be a complete . . .!! The Battalion was under canvas, and one blazing hot afternoon the C.S.M. was having a kip in his tent. His head made a bulge in the tent wall. A tent-peg mallet lay nearby. The combination proved too much for some passing soldier. When the C.S.M. came out of hospital, six months later, he was a changed man, so I was told! It was never officially discovered who wielded the mallet, but a batman I had, a long time afterwards, told me the soldier walked up and down for several minutes, in an agony of indecision, before he picked it up! It's a pity so many people have to learn the hard way.

Returning to the goose hanging in the tree; take it down whilst it is still warm and off to the wood-shed for a long plucking session. You aren't likely to get it done in under an hour, possibly considerably longer. The reason is that the whole job has to be done twice; first the outer layer of feathers and then the down underneath. The skin is tough, so you won't tear it, but you will find there is an awful large acreage of goose. Take the wings off at the elbow so that you do not have to pull out the pinions. It is difficult to explain, but instead of pulling the down out, you roll it out with the ball of your thumb, picking it up between the thumb and forefinger. Cut round the neck an inch or two above the shoulders, draw the skin back and cut the neck as close to the body as possible. Save the neck. Cut round below the heel joint, break the bone, and take off the paddles and tendons in the same way as for anything else. They need quite a pull. Now draw it. Open from the breast-bone to the vent and remove the lot. Save the liver, heart and gizzard. Cut away the vent, and check that the crop is empty and clean. Singe off the fluff over a gas or methylated spirit flame.

Sage and onion stuffing is the next job. Don't make the stodgy pud that many books give as S & OS. All sog and pretty little S & O! The inside of a goose is a large cave, and takes a lot of filling. You will need probably half a dozen large onions and a quarter of a loaf of bread. Buy your sage green in the late summer and hang it in small bunches from the ceiling in the kitchen to dry. The flavour is stronger and better than the powdered variety sold in jars. Peel the onions and cut them up into half-inch cubes, bring to the boil and cook for ten minutes. Drain the water off and tip into a bowl. Make the bread into crumbs. I find the easiest way is to cut off the crusts, slice in strips lengthways and then slice crossways, very finely. If it is new bread and you try to crumble it in your fingers, it will go into doughy lumps. Break a raw egg over the onion and sprinkle over the top some sage that you have ground up in the palm of your left hand with the heel of the thumb of your right. Scatter in a handful of breadcrumbs and start mixing. Go on adding more sage and breadcrumbs till the mixture begins to solidify. Put in pepper and salt and administer a final beating. The stuffing should be onion flavoured with sage, and held together by breadcrumbs and raw egg—not a lump of wet bread with a few bits of onion and sage dotted about in it. Stand the goose on its neck end and shovel the stuffing in. A little needle and cotton work may be necessary to close the abdominal cut, or the tying of the legs to the Pope's Nose may be enough when it is trussed. Put another tape or string round the body to hold the wings in.

Roast in about the same heat as you would use for mutton, starting hot and then falling away to medium. Some people scatter flour over the breast of the goose before putting in the oven with the idea that it makes the skin crisp and brown.

The apple sauce can be made at the same time as the bird is roasting. Peel and core two pounds of cooking apples (use Bramleys if you can). Slice them into a suitably sized bowl, scatter between 2-ozs. and a quarter pound of sugar over them, add four cloves and put the bowl in the oven with the goose. Take out and stir in half an hour. When the apple goes soft and transparent, add a large lump of butter, stir in and leave to cool. Apple sauce is much nicer cold or warm than it is hot.

It is almost impossible to tell you how long to cook your goose (literally). Size of bird and heat of oven vary too much. Go by looks to start with, and then confirm by cutting a leg free and pressing it out and down. If the hip-joint dislocates easily, the bird is cooked.

Make the gravy in the usual way. Pour off the goose-grease into a bowl, scatter in a spoonful of flour, stir and blend over the stove, pour in the correct amount of stock from the simmered giblets and boil till smooth. Keep the goose-grease. Its uses, according to tradition, are legion. The only ones I can think of at the moment are smearing it on your face to improve your complexion, and on your shooting boots to stop them leaking. I don't know about faces, but I can guarantee it for boots!

DUCKS

The dressing and cooking of the domestic duck is exactly the same as for goose, with the exception that duck is stuffed with oranges instead of sage and onion. Peel the oranges and either divide them into segments or slice them up. Stuff the duck tight with them. If you are feeling rich and want to create an impression, pour a glass of Grande Marnier over the bird and light it just as you bring it into the dining room. Most effective, and gives the skin a marvellous flavour. Another glass tipped into the stuffing doesn't do any harm either!

The wild ducks can either be excellent to eat or absolutely filthy—depending almost entirely on what they have been eating. Mallard is the largest, and the one people think of when Wild Duck is mentioned. The drake is a magnificent bird in full plumage, with his brilliant green head, blue and white speculum on the secondaries of the wing, and red legs. The duck, in her own way, is just as beautiful, her fawn and brown camouflage mottling making her almost invisible on her nest. Mallard and Teal are our main home-nesting species, most of the others coming in from the north in the autumn. Both of them are broad-minded when it comes to grub, but the Mallard is a real scavenger. Nothing comes amiss—grass, frogs, acorns, mice, Zostera grass, crabs, rabbit guts, black-berries, corn, winkles and water-beetles—down they all go. Until the corn is ripe they are feeding either in the ditches or on the shore, and I have come to the conclusion that it is a complete waste to shoot them at this time. They taste of the smell of a stirred up horse-pond and the only way you can eat them is for the duck to be stuffed with very strong sage and onion, and for you to have a cold in the head. But wait till the beginning of September, when they have been feeding on the lodged corn, and later on the stubbles, for a week or two. Shoot them then, as they flight in, in the evening, and out in the morning, and you will have something you can be proud to put on the table.

By the time the hard weather comes, after Christmas, most of our home-bred birds will have gone south to Spain and North Africa. The ones that are left will be foraging for what little food they can find on the seashore and will not be good to eat. During the winter. of 1962–3, when the cold was so intense, I had a Mallard and six ducks coming in to a spring in the field just below the farm to be fed morning and evening. I kept the ice broken on the little pond and fed them on mink food, which is a minced-up mixture of fish-offal, tripe, liver and meal, with sometimes a scattering of Indian corn. They got through a hundredweight of this fish-paste before the frost broke, and seemed to be in very good order at the end of it. A lot of duck died of starvation. It occurred to me that if anyone shot one of my ducks and tried to eat it, he would wish he hadn't! All of which boils down to the fact that the best time to eat Wild Duck is from the middle of September to the middle of December.

Teal are the smallest of the British ducks, being only a little over a foot long; and, as they are more inland-feeders than the other species, they are probably the best to eat. The drake has a chestnut head and a band of green running down the side of the head and neck from the eye. The speculum on the wing is bright, glossy green, and the mantle and flanks contain the barred black and white feathers that form the wing of such famous sea-trout flies as Teal & Silver and Peter Ross. The duck has the green speculum, but is otherwise dappled brown. Many of our home-bred birds winter in North Africa and the Nile Valley—where they live on a diet of rice. A Teal not only flies very fast "straight and level", but its rate and angle of climb are quite remarkable. Taking off from water they seem to have been rocketed into the air and it is very easy to shoot underneath them, especially when they explode out of a stream or creek almost under one's nose.

The winter after the Battle of Britain, the Squadron had a charming ex-Indian Army Colonel as Adjutant. Recalling these wise, experienced and diplomatic officers for service with the R.A.F. was a stroke of genius on somebody's part. This particular one treated us rather as a benevolent uncle would have done, and his hair must have been turned even whiter by his efforts—usually successful—to get us out of the frequent scrapes we got ourselves into. Indeed a pleasant change from his opposite number in the Army—Captain The Hon. Algernon Shrapnell-Bloodworthy—who had devilled Second Lieutenant on toast for breakfast most mornings!

One afternoon, when we were standing down, we took the Colonel shooting over the Stour marshes. The thaw had started, and a perishing wind blew across the saltings. Our flying-boots were sodden with the melting snow and mud, and it was getting dark. The total bag for the expedition was one big marsh hare. The Colonel had gone wandering off on his own a good hour ago, and there was still no sign of him. We were just about to dump the hare and go to look for him when we spotted a figure in the distance, plodding up the muddy edge of the river. Presently he came up. A fine-looking old boy he was—dark, piercing eye, bristling white moustache, and a terrible sabre cut right across one side of his face. "Hello Colonel, we were starting to think you'd fallen in." "No, my boy, no. Been lookin' for teal in the nallas." Some nallas!

The dressing and cooking of both mallard and teal is just the same, and very simple. Duck are eaten fresh, and should not be hung for more than a couple of days, except in very cold weather. Pluck, draw and truss as for goose, but do not stuff unless you think the birds may be "ditchy"—in which case either give them away to someone you don't particularly like or fill them with strong S & O. Wildfowl do not, as a rule, have much fat on them; so cover with fat bacon before roasting slowly. Baste frequently to prevent drying. Boil the giblets in the usual way, to provide stock for the gravy, and after you have put the flour in and finished making it except for its final boil, grate a little orange-peel in as well. When serving the duck, put one or two small plates of orange segments on the table. I would suggest creamed potato and Brussels sprouts.

WIGEON

Wigeon is the only other British duck that occurs in quantities great enough for it to be of culinary importance. It is a shore and estuary duck, rarely coming inland, but because its diet is entirely vegetable it is good to eat. The drake may be distinguished by his chestnut head and neck contrasting with the light buff forehead and crown; bill leaden coloured, tipped with black; speculum green tipped with black. The rest of the body is mostly greyish. The local wildfowlers call them Whistling Duck. The call is very easily recognised—that of the drake being "Whee oo", a musical whistling sound. The ducks make a purring, growling noise. Both these calls are made when the birds are on the ground.

Wigeon should be plucked and drawn as soon as possible after they are shot, as the Zostera grass on which they mainly feed decomposes very rapidly and will discolour and spoil the bird unless the entrails are removed. Dressing and cooking are the same as for Mallard and Teal.

Whilst we are about it, I had better give you a list of the duck that you can eat, if you happen to shoot an odd one; and a list of those that you definitely can't eat—unless of course you are cast away on a desert island, and then you won't be unduly fussy!

Edible: Gadwall, Shoveler (sometimes), Garganey, Pintail (sometimes), Pochard, and possibly Tufted-duck.

Inedible: Eider, Golden-eye, Longtail, Shelduck, Scoter; also the Sawbill family, which comprises Goosander, Merganser and Smew.

At this point I must give you the classic receipt for the preparation and cooking of a Cormorant:

Having shot your cormorant, hold it well away from you as you carry it home; these birds are exceedingly verminous and the lice are said to be not entirely host-specific. Hang up by the feet with a piece of wire, soak in petrol and set on fire. This treatment both removes most of the feathers and kills the lice. When the smoke has cleared away, take the cormorant down and cut off the beak. Send this to the local Conservancy Board who, if you are in the right area, will give you 3/6d. or sometimes 5/- for it. Bury the carcase, preferably in a light sandy soil, and leave it there for a fortnight. This is said to improve the flavour by removing, in part at least, the taste of rotting fish. Dig up and skin and draw the bird. Place in a strong salt and water solution and soak for forty-eight hours. Remove, dry, stuff with whole, unpeeled onions—the onion skins are supposed to bleach the meat to a small extent, so that it is very dark brown instead of being entirely black. Simmer gently in sea-water, to which two tablespoons of chloride of lime have been added, for six hours. This has a further tenderising effect. Take out of the water and allow to dry, meanwhile mixing up a stiff paste of methylated spirit and curry powder. Spread this mixture liberally over the breast of the bird. Finally roast in a very hot oven for three hours. The result is unbelievable. Throw it away. Not even a starving vulture could eat it.

Before we leave the subject of ducks, I will give you what I consider to be one of the best, if not *the* best, way of cooking them:

Salmi of Duck can be used for a bird beyond its first year as well as for a young one. Roast the duck in the usual way, but roast in a higher heat and remove from the oven when the skin is crisp and brown but the meat is still pink and underdone. Cut it up into handy-sized pieces—the legs making two bits each, and the breast four. The best way of cutting up the breast is to slice down one side of the centre with a sharp knife and then follow up with poultry-shears or tin-snips for the bone. Do the same thing, crossways, to divide into quarters. Don't forget to take the little ear-shaped pieces out of the oyster-bones, in the middle of the back. These are supposed to be the only part of a bird that the Roman Emperors would condescend to eat; apart, of course, from peacock's brains! Put the remains of the carcase in the stock-pot.

Whilst the duck was roasting you were not, of course, sitting in front of the fire, with your feet on the mantelpiece, reading the paper! You were making half a pint of Espagnole sauce (see Cutlets, page 116), boiling a quarter-pound of button mushrooms in salted water for five minutes and collecting up half a pound of ordinary mushrooms, a claret-glass of port (and don't make the mistake that I did with the hare—see that it *is* "Produce of Portugal") some fresh apricots or peaches —or if too late in the season, tinned pineapple rings and, finally, a bottle of Cumberland Sauce. If no C.S., then the juice of an orange and some of the rind, grated. Pour the port into the pan with the Espagnole sauce, stir and heat up to the point where you can just taste it without burning your mouth. Shake the Cumberland sauce bottle up and start adding it, a dessertspoon at a time, stirring and tasting between times, till you have got as much orangy flavour as you want. Adjust the salt and pepper balance. Put the duck and the ordinary mushrooms in a casserole, pour the sauce over them, cover, and cook slowly for three-quarters of an hour. At the end of this time, take it out and prod to see if it is tender. Continue simmering and prodding until it *is* tender. Before serving, garnish with the button mushrooms and apricots (duly stoned and sliced) and also, if you like, croutons—which are small triangles of fried bread.

Exactly the same technique is used for *Salmi of Pheasant,* and an excellent way it is for cooking an old warrior. The only difference is that red-currant jelly is used in the sauce instead of Cumberland sauce or orange—but again it is the flavourings you yourself like that matter. This dish gives a lot of scope for experimenting. You can flavour it with metal-polish and garnish it with gunpowder—see if I care!

TURKEY

It may not happen for many years yet, but you are bound to get saddled with it in the end—Cooking the Turkey! Your mother went down with 'flu on December 23rd; your sister ran off with "that nice farm student from Bishops Strumpet" last week. And now, to crown everything, as your wife was putting the fairy on top of the Christmas tree, the steps slipped and now she's in bed with a busted collar-bone. Guess who's going to deal with Christmas dinner? "Daddy, may I have another sweetie, please?" "Daddy, do you remember, Rusty stole the ham-skin this afternoon?" "Yes." "Well he's just been sick under the dining-room table." "Daddy, what was in that big box you brought in this morning?" "The Doctor's car has just driven into the yard, Daddy." "Daddy, Grannie wants a cup of tea." "We don't need to go to bed *yet*, do we Daddy?" The 'phone starts ringing—wrong number. "Daddy, Susie's got her finger stuck up the wash-basin tap." "Daddy . . . Daddy . . . Daddy. . . ." Finally, you start leaping about and bellowing like a wounded bull. They all melt away, and you are left to your turkey.

The turkey will at least be plucked—if it isn't I have not the slightest sympathy for you!—and also probably drawn, but in the event of the latter being undone, it will only take you ten minutes to do it. If the feet are still on, draw the tendons in the same way as you do for a pheasant. And it takes some doing, too. I take mine to the workshop and put the foot in the vice. Then I put my foot against the vice and pull.

Save the neck, gizzard, heart and liver to make stock and turkey soup. Some people even used to go to the trouble of making giblet pie, but I don't think this is done much now-adays.

Most of the work attached to turkey-roasting is the making of the stuffings and trimmings. A turkey is best stuffed both fore and aft; forcemeat or sausage in the crop end, and sage and onion in the cave. As Veal Forcemeat is given under Beef Olives on page 103, I will put the Sausage stuffing receipt in now. I prefer it for this purpose anyhow.

Stuffing

Check to see that the crop of the bird has been properly removed, and then cram the whole front end as tight as you can with the following mixture:

    1-lb. pork sausage meat (unseasoned)
    ¼-lb. chopped ham or bacon
    1 breakfast-cup of fresh breadcrumbs
    1 large onion, chopped finely
    1 heaped tablespoon of parsley
    Grated rind of half a lemon
    Small teaspoon of mixed herbs
    2 raw eggs
    Pepper and salt.

Mix this lot together thoroughly in a large bowl, then prop the turkey up on its stern and fill up the crop. It will probably need a bit of stitching to keep all secure.

Sage and onion stuffing is included earlier in this chapter in the instructions on Goose, page 25.

You may find that it is unpractical to skewer right through in the "wing/leg, leg/wing" manner used for pheasant because of all the stuffing; so just tie the drumsticks to the Pope's Nose in the usual way, and then tie a tape round the body to keep the wings in place. Your bird should now look, and weigh, twice the turkey it did when you started. Put it away in the larder—well out of Rusty's reach!

Having now broken the back of Christmas dinner you can pour yourself a drink and have a short rest before you begin collecting up all the knick-knacks and gubbins to be wrapped in tissue paper and fed into stockings! Remind yourself, at frequent intervals, that this is a Time of Peace and Goodwill towards Men (nothing about women you'll notice!)—especially when you've just upset little Tommy's box of 500 air-gun slugs all over the floor.

You are awakened in the morning at 0500 hrs. just in time to have the same air-gun slugs tipped into your bed by a screaming Red Indian. Happy Christmas, chum!

The difficulty in roasting a turkey is always to cook the legs properly without drying out the breast to such an extent that it is spoiled. All too often when a magnificent bird is carved, the breast is the only part fit to eat, the legs being pink and almost raw. I have found the best way of overcoming the problem is this: Arm yourself with a pound of the fattest bacon you can buy, cut a quarter inch thick, and a roll of wide cooking foil. Cover the entire breast with bacon, overlapping it like the slates on a roof, including, of course, the bulge of stuffing at the front. This will not only keep it basted but will insulate and protect it from the heat. The legs, being exposed to all the heat there is, will cook faster; and so, if you roast slowly, the whole lot should be properly done at the same time. A kind of handicapping, really. Unroll some of the foil on the table, and put the bird on it, six inches from the end. Fold the foil up all round to form a sort of dish. Bring the roll back over the top and cut off six inches beyond the bird. Fold this into a lid, fitting over the dish. In this way most of the steam and fat vapour is retained to moisten and baste the bird.

Remember, once the turkey is stuffed it is no longer a hollow shell, but a solid block which needs long, slow cooking. Supposing the total weight of the bird, stuffings and all, were fifteen pounds, it will take around four hours of "just sizzling" cooking somewhere, I suppose, in the 350-400° F. range. For the last three-quarters of an hour, remove the foil and the bacon from the top and step the heat up to brown the skin nicely. Baste once during this time. Take out of the roasting tin, put on the carving dish and place in the warm oven till needed.

The usual trimmings that go with turkey are chipolata sausages, bread sauce, bacon rolls, Brussels sprouts and creamed potatoes. The Americans eat cranberry sauce with their turkey at one of their jollifications—Independence Day or something. Quite good it is, too.

You will find instructions for Bread Sauce and Bacon Rolls under Roast Pheasant on page 8. Pour off the fat from the roasting tin, and make the gravy in the usual manner.

If there are any children around, using up the rest of the bird cold won't present any problem! And scraps, pickings off the carcase, etc. can be minced, mixed with mashed spud, a little chopped raw onion and a pinch of herbs; coat with egg and breadcrumbs and fry. Croquettes to the refeened, rissoles to the earthy!

Devilled Drumsticks and bacon make a very pleasant breakfast for the Master. So issue a directive to the effect that neither the Wolf-pack nor Rusty are to get their slavering jaws on the drumsticks.

The diabolical mixture consists of:

1-oz. butter
¼-teaspoon each of Cayenne pepper, curry powder, black pepper
Pinch of ginger.

Mix thoroughly ("Light the blue touch paper and stand well back") and spread on the drumsticks, which have previously been scored with deep longitudinal cuts. The mixture needs time to soak into the meat, so do the preparation the night before. Fry or grill till browned and very hot, and eat with bacon and fried bread. Have a breakfast-cup of coffee ready to put the fire out.

CHICKEN

Chicken is rather a problem these days. At a large professional conference not long ago, the representative of one of the main poultry-food manufacturers got up and said: "We have found how to feed broilers so that they grow fast and resist disease, but we wish someone could tell us how to make them taste of chicken." It is very doubtful whether any method will ever be found which will produce a table bird, or an egg, which can compare with those raised by the traditional free-range system. I think it was Coke of Norfolk who said "If you stick to Nature when you go afarming m'boy, you won't go far wrong." The old gentleman will be gyrating in his grave, never mind turning, if he can see the things being done to land and livestock these days. Poison insecticides, poison weed-killers, artificial fertilisers, pellet-feeding and antibiotics—to mention but a few. What the eventual result will be is on the knees of the Gods, but many eminent men in the fields of medicine, ecology, botany and zoology are very concerned at the present trend. They might as well dismiss the matter from their minds.

Nothing will ever be done about it, even if these things are proved to be harmful. Too many people are cashing in.

Have you ever watched cattle turned into a new field that has been heavily dressed with one of the nitrogenous artificials —sulphate of ammonia, nitrate of soda or nitro-chalk? The grass is lush-looking and emerald green; but the cattle, after a mouthful or two, will go to the hedgerows or dykes and eat the grasses and herbs which have been naturally nourished by the fall of the leaves each autumn. Only when this is all finished will they start on the other. They have no alternative. The battery hen in her cage eats the pellets which are provided for her, and for the same reason. As long as the public will go on buying the primrose-yolked, watery-whited rubbish that she lays, she will stay there.

And now there is talk of battery beef. There are many exceptions of course, but taking them by and large, farmers are just about as callous and selfish a body of men as you could well find. That jolly, bucolic, animal-loving character Farmer Giles is, I'm afraid, largely a myth. The way some of them treat their women, children, hands and dogs would make even Captain Bligh blink. I heard one of them in a pub, not long ago, bemoaning the fact that there did not seem much likelihood of another war in the immediate future—so that he could make another fortune. Had I broken a bottle over his head, as he richly deserved, *I* would have been the one to be hauled off to clink. There's no justice! When you think of it, there never was.

Whilst I agree that a lot of codswallop is talked about the longing of the battery hen for the wide open spaces, there should be a limit to the exploitation by one section of the community of another section, whether human or animal, for financial gain. If farm stock, whether animal, avian, or vegetable, can be grown under conditions as reasonably near to nature as possible, and with the added benefits of good husbandry, the end product will be of as high a quality as it is possible to achieve. Not only that: the cow, sheep, hen or cabbage will have *enjoyed* its brief spell on earth. The modern trend towards incarceration and artificial feeding, whilst it lines the farmers' pockets with even more gold, does nothing for the quality of the produce and is a retrogressive step towards the days of "the dark Satanic mills".

Following on from all this, and bearing in mind the old saying that most of us have had chucked at us when we were kids: "If you want a thing done properly, do it yourself", it would seem that the only way of getting top quality eggs, table poultry and vegetables is to grow them oneself—or buy them from someone else who does.

ROAST CHICKEN

Having grown or bought a good cock-chicken, treat it exactly as you would a very small turkey, except that the front end is not stuffed with sausage-meat. It has always been customary to stuff chicken with sage and onion in this part of the country. I like it. It not only adds to the flavour, but it also helps to prevent drying-out. Make bread-sauce and bacon rolls, a good gravy, Brussels sprouts and creamed potato, and there are few better meals.

CHICKEN & MUSHROOM PIE

This is, I think, the best way of using an old bird. It is also a useful party dish, because all the work is done beforehand and all you need to do is shove it in the oven (heated in readiness) for half an hour, whilst you are giving your guests a drink. Of course the services of Flakey Flossie, the pastry-girl, will be required; but you ought to have got her properly organised by now! (See Rabbit Pie, page 55).

Pluck and draw the hen in the usual manner, then take off the legs and, with shears and a knife, cut the carcase in half lengthways—along one side of the breastbone and the spine. Flour these joints and fry them to a golden brown colour. Peel and chop two large onions. Fry them in olive oil, scattering a couple of dessertspoons of flour in as you turn them, till transparent and beginning to colour. Put the hen and the onion in a big pot or casserole, with the giblets and seasoning, and cook until the meat can easily be taken off the bones. In the meanwhile you have fried a quarter-pound of bacon and cut it into smallish pieces, hardboiled three or four eggs, and prepared the mushrooms. If they are small buttons, you can put them in whole—stalk and all—but if they are larger, then cut them into suitably sized bits.

Take the joints out of the stewpan one by one, put them on a meat dish, so that you will have room to manoeuvre, and remove all the meat from the bones. Put the wreckage in the stock-pot. Get your pie-dish and put in alternate layers of chicken, quartered, hardboiled egg, bacon and mushrooms, until the dish is full. Strain the gravy from the stewpan and top the pie-dish up with it. Put in the larder to cool. Phone Flossie and tell her to start warming her engines up. The only further cooking that the pie requires is the time needed for the pastry. This will be sufficient to cook the mushrooms and blend the flavours. Put some herbs in if you like, and alter the seasoning till you find a balance that suits you. A glass of dry white wine in the gravy, or a little dry sherry, doesn't come amiss.

As this is supposed to be a cookery book as opposed to a recipe book, I will leave you to find Chicken Maryland, etc. elsewhere.

WOODCOCK & SNIPE

Woodcock and Snipe are both valued among shooting men for the exceedingly difficult and sporting shots they provide.

Woodcock, as its name indicates, is almost always put up in coppice-woods and other thick cover. Its owl-like, twisting flight as it swerves away through the trees makes it much more often missed than hit. Most of the woodcock that are shot during the season are migrants from Scandinavia, but there is also a small resident population that nests here. The camouflage of these birds sitting on their nests, is quite amazing. One of the dogs put a hen off her nest last April. I saw her get up and went to look. A little hollow scooped in the dead oak leaves contained four eggs. I marked exactly where it was, and went back the next day to see that she was all right. I moved up, very slowly, to within a couple of yards of the nest and looked—and looked! So perfectly did she blend with her background that I could not distinguish her until I spotted her beady black eye, watching me. A spring evening wouldn't be the same without woodcock and snipe. When the hen woodcock is sitting, the cock does a patrol from dusk till dark. Known as "roding" or "roading" it consists of a triangular course around, or over, the wood where the nest is. Flying at about fifty feet, he comes over the same route every time, and as he flies he makes an odd snoring noise punctuated with high-pitched squeaks. Occasionally they both fly together, making a twittering sound, but probably this is before the hen is "sitting hard". The snipe's contribution to the evening—drumming—is a bit of a mystery. Nobody knows for certain how the sound is made, but most authorities agree that it is caused by the wind vibrating in the outer feathers of the out-spread tail during a fairly steep dive. A noise more like a sheep bleating than anything else, it is more often heard when the light has almost gone. Snipe are rather like woodcock to look at, only much smaller. Long legs, long beaks, and brown and fawn mottled plumage. The pin-feathers (a little pointed feather on the leading edge of the wing, just at the base of the first primary) of both species have been used by painters for doing very delicate work since time immemorial.

From a gastronomic viewpoint, woodcock and snipe are both very highly prized by the epicure. Traditionally, they are plucked, head and all; the head is twisted round and they are skewered with their own beaks. They are not drawn, but the eyes are usually removed. After this they are spread with butter, covered with bacon, and roasted. Personally, I find this method aesthetically displeasing. It makes a very fine bird look stupid—and I like my game drawn.

I would advise hanging woodcock for a reasonable time, taking into account the temperature, as the ones I have eaten fresh have always been rubbery. Snipe can be eaten either way. Pluck, dress and draw in the usual way, cover with bacon and roast, on a piece of toast, in the same way as plover.

Many dogs will avoid picking up snipe and woodcock if they can get away with it; and if I offer any of my own spaniels a piece of cooked snipe, woodcock or curlew, they will give it one sniff and look at me as if to say: "You don't expect me to eat that filthy stuff, do you?" Which makes me think, when I find them munching up the most appalling lumps of rotting carrion with evident relish!

I cannot leave the subject of wildfowl without giving you some of the opinions and observations of that almost legendary character and sportsman, Lt.-Col. Peter Hawker. A cavalry officer under Sir Arthur Wellesley, in the years leading up to Waterloo, he won for his regiment (the 14th Light Dragoons) the battle-honour "Douro" in 1808. The same year he received a wound in the thigh which resulted in his being gazetted out of the army in 1813. This probably saved his life, and also made possible the writing of the most original and fascinating book on shooting that is ever likely to be printed: *Instructions to Young Sportsmen in All that Relates to Guns and Shooting*. As this book is exceedingly difficult to come by, in any edition or reprint, I will quote you the gallant colonel's advice to the sportsman who is about to set up his shooting headquarters in a country inn of that period:

> "As many of the little publicans live chiefly on fat pork and tea; or, if on the coast, red herrings; the experienced traveller well knows that, when in a retired place of this sort, where, from the very circumstance of the misery attending it, there are the fewer sportsmen, and consequently, there is to be had the best diversion, we have often to depend a little on our wits for procuring the necessaries of life. If even a nobleman (who is, of course, by common people, thought in the greatest extreme better than a gentleman without a title) were to enter an alehouse, the most that could be procured for him would be mutton or beef, both perhaps as tough, and with as little fat, as the boots or gaiters on his legs. A chop or steak is provided. If he does not eat it, he may starve; if he does, his pleasure for the next day is possibly destroyed by his unpleasant sufferings from indigestion. He gets some sour beer, which gives him the heartburn, and probably calls for brandy or gin; the one execrably bad and unwholesome, the other of the worst quality; and *of course* mixed with water, by which adulteration is derived the greatest part of the publican's profit. The spirit merchants make it, what they call above

proof, in order to allow for its being *diluted*, the doing which, so far from dishonest, is now the common practice, not only with many respectable innkeepers, but by retail merchants themselves. Our young sportsman, at last, retires to a miserable chamber and a worse bed; where, for want of ordering it to be properly aired, he gets the rheumatism; and, from the draughts of air that penetrate the room, he is attacked with the toothache. He rises to a breakfast of bad tea, without milk; and then starts for his day's sport, so (to use a fashionable term) 'bedevilled' that he cannot 'touch a feather', and in the evening, returns to his second edition of misery.

"On the other hand, the old campaigner would, under such circumstances, do tolerably well, and have his complete revenge on the fish or fowl of the place.

"His plan, knowing the improbability of getting anything to eat, would be to provide himself with a hand-basket at the last country town he had to pass through, before he reached his exile; and then stock it with whatever good things presented themselves. He then arrives at the pothouse, which the distance, or the badness of the roads, might oblige him to do the previous day. His first order is for his sheets and bedding to be put before a good fire. If he arrives too late at night for this let him, rather than lie between sheets which are not properly aired, sleep with only the blankets. He then, supposing he would not be at the trouble of carrying meat, sends for his beef or mutton. Having secured this for the *next* day's dinner, he takes out of his basket something ready dressed, or some eggs, or a string of sausages, or a few kidneys; or a fowl to boil, a cake or two of portable soup, or a little mock turtle, ready to warm; or, in short, any other things that the town may have afforded; and with this, he makes up his dinner on the day of his arrival. If the beer is sour, and he does not choose to be troubled with carrying bottles of other beverage, he is provided with little *carbonate of soda*, which will correct the acid; a little nutmeg or powdered ginger, to take off the unpleasant taste; and with a spoonful of brown sugar and a toast, he will make tolerably palatable that which, before, was scarce good enough to quench the thirst.

"He will know better than to call for brandy or gin, but will order *rum*, knowing that this is a spirit which would soon be spoiled by any tricks or adulteration. He will have in his basket some lemons, or a bottle of lemon acid, and will make a bowl of punch, recollecting the proportions of

> One sour
> Two sweet
> Four strong
> And eight weak.

This is quite the focus for good punch, which any shallow-headed boy may remember, by learning it as a bad rhyme. "It may be necessary to observe that, by first pounding the sugar fine, you can of course measure it to a nicety, by means of a wineglass, as well as the lemon juice, and the other liquids. Also, that half the acid of a Seville orange is better than all of lemon juice; and further, in making punch, the spirit should be used as the finishing ingredient; though put in another jug; and the SHERBET POURED UPON IT."

I had always thought that Sherbert was that fizzy powder I used to buy at the tuck-shop when I was a small boy, so I looked it up in a 1907 Chambers's Dictionary:

"SHERBET A drink of water and fruit juices, sweetened and flavoured (From the Turkish)".

The receipt that Col. Hawker gives is for a hot punch.

In case you want to make a Napoleonic Punch for some special Winter party, I will simplify the foregoing instructions:

Put, in an enamel saucepan, the following ingredients:

One wineglass of lemon juice (or half a wineglass of Seville orange juice)

Two wineglasses of castor sugar

Eight wineglasses of water.

Bring this mixture to the boil, stirring occasionally. Take off the heat and allow to cool for five minutes (so that it will neither crack the jug nor vapourise the alcohol) and then pour on to the four glasses of rum, which you have previously put in a jug. Stir up and pour out.

And finally:

"Let me now add the simple receipt for as wholesome a mess as anyone who can rough it would wish for—the dinner, of all others, for an invalid—and an alternative against starvation, where there is not even a piece of meat to be got.

Have a fowl skinned and quartered
Put it over the fire in a quart of cold water
Boil it *full two hours*
Then add two ounces (or a handful) of pearl barley
Three blades of mace; about two dozen peppercorns; and
Salt to your taste;
Then let *all* boil *together* for *one more* hour

And it may be eat immediately; or put by, to warm again whenever you want it.

"The convenience of this camp cooking is, that it will serve for any kind of fowl. For instance, if you have an old barn-door hen; old game that is all shot to pieces; two or three couple of gulls; coots; or even curlews—by consigning them in this manner, to constant boiling and steam, you make those birds eatable and digestible, which, in roasting or common cooking, would prove offensive in taste, and hard in substance."

Hawker, by the way, uses both "receipt" and "recipe" quite impartially.

* ✿ * ✿ * ✿ * ✿ * ✿ * ✿ *

PART TWO

* ✿ * ✿ * ✿ * ✿ * ✿ * ✿ *

Hare

Rabbit

* ✹ *

CHAPTER V

HARE

HARE, strangely enough, does not seem to be a particularly popular dish these days. Shooting men have difficulty in finding people to give their hares away to, and the poulterers in the towns sell them for a few shillings—if they can get rid of them at all. It is usually the older country people who will welcome this gift, and I suspect that, except for them, the knowledge of how to prepare and cook a hare has almost died out.

The preparation of a hare is equally as important as the cooking, if not more so. Hanging, as usual, is a matter of personal preference. At the beginning of the season, when the weather is warm, five to seven days should be enough; and in January three weeks would not be too much. A hare is hung "as it is"—not drawn. Why a rabbit must be "paunched" at once to prevent it going rotten, and a hare can be hung for weeks and only become more "gamey", has always been a mystery to me—but it is so.

Take your hare out of the larder, provide yourself with a large plate or bowl, a small bowl, and a sharp knife. Choose a place where you can make a gory mess without having too much trouble cleaning it up afterwards, and set to work. Make a long cut down the belly, cutting only through the "pelt" and not the abdominal wall. This is tricky but well worth doing carefully. From this cut, make two more down the insides of the hind legs to the hocks—these are easy because it doesn't matter if you cut a little way into the muscle. By working the pelt away from the meat, and a bit of pulling and tugging, skin out the hind legs. Now put a meat hook through the "ham-strings" (hocks, Achilles tendons, or whatever you like to call them) and hang up. Pull the skin down to the front legs and draw them out, cutting off at the wrists. Another pull will expose the neck; cut a circle round this at right angles and then twist the head round a couple of times. It will come off. Take the carcase down and lay it on its back.

Now, with a sharp, heavy knife, open up the rib cage from the V (solar plexus) of the ribs to the neck, cutting slightly to one side of centre as this is easier. Push your knife in and slit the diaphragm in several places. Put the small bowl on the floor, carefully pick up the hare and pour the blood out of it, supporting the hare with both hands and treating the operation rather as if you were pouring from one bowl into another. The object of the exercise is to get the maximum of blood into the bowl and the minimum on yourself and the floor! It is possible to end up with a mess which Ghengis Khan himself couldn't better! Put the bowl of blood where you won't kick it over, and draw the hare—saving the liver and heart; to do this, simply slit the belly open and remove the lot. Remove the gall-bladder from the liver. This is a greenish-grey bag situated in a cleft in the liver. Take it between the finger and thumb and peel it off, from the thick end, upwards. Throw away.

Unless you want to roast your hare (of which, more later) you now joint it. Place it on its front with the hindquarters towards you. Cut round the two arcs where the hind legs join the pelvis. Turn over and cut along the insides of the legs, exposing the ball and socket joints of the thigh bones. Sever the ligaments, holding them together, and remove the legs. They should look like rather elongated hams. Cut round at right angles immediately above the hip bones and twist the pelvis off. Throw it away, because in either hare or rabbit it will spoil the flavour of your dish. Cutting up and in below the bottom ribs on each side, take off the back in the same way. Run your knife under the shoulder-blades and remove the front legs—they are only held on with muscle. Take the feet off the hind legs by cutting the ham-strings, dislocating the joints, and cutting the ligaments. You will notice that the hare has been *jointed* and that no bones have been broken. Trying to eat hare, or rabbit, that has been hacked up with a cleaver is worse than cherry pie! There is no need to wash the joints unless you have dropped them on the floor or got them covered in fur. Either burn or bury the skin and guts very deep or your dog will certainly dig them up and eat them, thereby catching tapeworm, with which they are almost always infested.

Hare is a rich meat but also a very dry one and so is better cooked as some form of stew or casserole. Roast hare is not a good idea. I have eaten both other people's efforts and my own—larded and basted—and I have to admit that not only does the end product look like an Egyptian mummified cat but is, I should imagine, just about as stringy. However, as the Actress said to the Bishop "There's no accounting for tastes!"

There are two basic receipts for hare that I have found excellent. The first is more or less the traditional Jugged Hare, which is used for a hare that has been hung for some time. The other, which gives an entirely different flavour, is for those who do not care for the richness of the first, or for use as a change from it.

JUGGED HARE

Make a marinade—which is simply another name for the liquid in which meats are soaked—of draught cider (preferably dry, but medium sweet will do), thinly-sliced raw onion, freshly-ground black pepper, and salt. Put the joints of hare and the liver in it and leave them overnight. The object in doing this is not only to put flavour into the dish, but to make it tender. Cider has a remarkable property of being able to break down meat. In fact, a lump of beef in a vat of cider will disappear completely if left long enough! One pint of cider and one medium onion should be enough.

Twelve hours will be sufficient time for a young hare to stay in the marinade, but an old one could do with twenty-four. Take the joints out and dry them, roll them in flour and then fry them in olive oil (preferably) till golden brown. Put them in a casserole or a thick iron pot, tip the marinade in and top up with water till covered. Add a teaspoon of thyme if you like. Bring to the boil in the oven and then simmer very gently till the meat leaves the bones easily when prised off. Do not cook till it falls off on its own. The time varies, but usually one and a half to two and a half hours according to the age of the hare.

Now get out a large meat dish and your larger covered glass casserole. Take the joints out one by one and remove the meat from them. This is most conveniently done on a big dish, where the wreckage can be pushed to the far end. Place the meat in the casserole. Chop the liver up finely and put it in too.

The gravy is one of the most important parts of the dish. Strain the cooking liquor into a suitably-sized saucepan and boil it away till you consider that you have the right amount comfortably to cover the meat. Whilst it is boiling "despumate" it—in other words, skim off the scum and grease which rises to the top. Melt a tablespoon of redcurrant jelly in it. Now get the bowl of blood. With a spoon, ladle some gravy into the bowl and stir, adding more till you have a smooth mixture. Tip this into the saucepan and stir until the gravy thickens. Heat it up a little if you wish, but do not let it boil, or you will have blood-curdled gravy! Finally, add a glass of port—reasonable port, not British port-style. I did this once and completely ruined my hare. A false economy. Pour the gravy over the meat and put in a warm oven until needed.

Creamed potatoes and any winter vegetable you prefer—sprouts, leeks or carrots, go well with this dish. Many receipts will tell you to make forcemeat balls. These are very nice, but a lot of trouble, so unless you are afraid there will not be enough to feed the company, I should not bother with them.

HARE WITH LEMON JUICE

This method is not only useful for people who do not like Jugged Hare, but it can also be applied when the hare has been so badly shot up that it is impossible to hang it for more than a couple of days.

As soon as possible after the hare is shot, paunch it (open up the belly and remove all the entrails). Hang for two days to a week, according to the weather. Skin and joint as for jugged hare.

Prepare a marinade of the juice of four lemons, onion, black pepper and salt. Soak for twelve to twenty-four hours, according to the age of the hare. As there will not be enough liquid to cover the joints, they should be turned in the marinade when you remember to do so.

Flour and fry, as in the previous receipt, and then casserole, using boiling water as the cooking liquor. The amount of the marinade to include depends on personal taste. If all the lemon juice is poured in, the dish will have a definitely tart flavour, so experiment until you arrive at the right amount. Cook until the meat leaves the bones fairly easily as you take it off. Strain the cooking liquor into another saucepan; boil down and skim off the grease. Adjust the flavouring with garlic, herbs, parsley, etc. as you think fit. A glass of sherry stirred in at the last moment is a good idea. Serve redcurrant jelly on the table instead of putting it in the gravy. Pour over the meat and keep hot until wanted. Boil it again if you like—it will do no harm, as the blood has not been used.

❀

RABBIT

RABBIT was, before Hitler's War, the staple dish in the country. Whilst not perhaps as versatile as the pig, it could be turned into pies, stews, fricassées, curries, etc. etc., which could just as easily have been made of chicken or turkey.

Undoubtedly rabbits did do a lot of damage to crops and gardens, but this, in the majority of cases, was largely the farmers' own fault. With the exception of those whose land marched with large areas of heath or forestry land, to which the farmer did not have access and which were swarming with rabbits, the farmer could control his rabbits and, at the same time, make a profit on them. Some even paid their rent in this way. I have happy memories of a large Yorkshire farm where I was a student in the early 'thirties. We had just moved in, and it fairly hopped with rabbits. There was a 30-acre field with woods of some 20-odd acres each on either side of it. The rabbits lived in the woods and came out in thousands to feed in the field. The technique we perfected was this: Long-nets (bought and borrowed from anywhere and everywhere) were set along the edges of the woods, looped up so that the rabbits could come out under them into the field. These were left for a couple of days so that the rabbits would get used to them, and then on Der Tag (a suitable warm, rabbity night!) the cords would be quietly pulled, and the net would fall. Two men were detailed to look after each net when the circus started. The farmer had a magnificent 1928 3-litre Sunbeam —an open tourer. We took it in turns—but usually he drove and I stood beside him in the space where the passenger's seat went—with a .410 shot gun. A lad was standing on each running-board—hanging on—whilst the car swept down into the big field with its headlamps full on. Rabbits everywhere! But not easy shots by any means. The lads jumped off, picked up the casualties, put them in the back of the car, and jumped on again. Whilst this caper was going on, hundreds of rabbits were heading for the woods and charging into the nets.

It took a long time to paunch and leg two or three hundred rabbits, but they made an imposing sight, hanging up to cool before they went into market the following morning.

The Depression was by no means over, and people were only too pleased to be able to buy good meat at a reasonable price. The felt manufacturers bought most of the skins to make hats. Besides this, landowners were able to pay their keepers' wages out of the rabbits they trapped during the winter; and a shooting tenant reckoned on paying at least half his rent out of the rabbits. In view of this, it is difficult to see who has gained from the barbarous extermination of the rabbit by myxomatosis and cyanide gas. Apart from the practical loss all round, it is diabolical deliberately to infect any animal with so filthy a disease as myxomatosis. However, in this Jack-in-office society, I might as well save my breath to cool my porridge!

As soon as possible after the rabbit is dead it should be paunched—slit from the end of the sternum down to the bottom of the abdomen—and the entrails removed. Examine the liver; if this looks at all doubtful—discoloured, blotchy or ragged— discard the rabbit. If, by mistake, you have shot a doe feeding a litter, she will only be fit to feed the dogs. *A propos* of this, it is useful to remember that the large rabbit you see feeding by day, and usually by itself, is almost always a doe with a big litter to feed. So spare her, unless she is guzzling in your vegetable garden.

Having paunched the rabbit you "leg" it and hang it in your game larder. "Legging" consists of cutting a slit between the ham-string and the bone on one hind leg and then pushing the other hind foot through beyond the heel, so that a loop is formed by which to hang the carcase up. If rabbits are wanted in couples, you simply put the hind foot of one rabbit through the loop of the already legged one, fasten together, and you have "a couple of rabbits" which can be hung over a pole or a fence, without the need for string or hooks.

Skinning and dressing a rabbit is exactly the same as for a hare, only very much easier. Work the pelt and the carcase apart just above the pelvis, skin out the hind legs, pull the pelt up till the shoulder blades are exposed, skin out the front legs, cut the head off. Joint in the same way too—hind legs off, cut just above the hip bones, twist the pelvis off and *throw it away*. This is most important, as the unpleasant rabbity flavour that puts people off this meat is produced by including the pelvis in the stew. Cut the back section into two pieces, and then you can, at a pinch, feed four—two with a hind leg each and the others with a joint of back and front leg apiece. The rib cage is only included to help make stock, and should not be served.

I will give three basic receipts. These can, of course, be varied and altered indefinitely.

RABBIT CASSEROLE

Wash the joints in cold water and then place in a marinade of draught cider, thinly-sliced onion, salt and pepper for about twelve hours. Alternatively, put in plain salt and water for the same length of time. Remove the pieces, dry and flour them. Peel and cut up two medium onions into half-inch cubes. Fry these in olive oil and, before you turn them in the pan, sprinkle a dessertspoon of flour over them. Turn and cook till transparent and slightly golden. Place in the casserole. A strange property of onion is the way its taste changes enormously according to the amount of cooking it receives. Using raw onion, "fried till transparent" onion or "fried till going crisp" will give your dish three different flavours.

Now fry the rabbit golden and place on top of the onion. Pack in the spaces with carrot—new ones, of course, are the best but otherwise old ones sliced in quarter-inch discs. If you have used cider to marinade, pour this in and top up with water; otherwise, cover with boiling water. Add salt, cayenne pepper, black pepper, two cloves of garlic, thyme or marjoram —severally or collectively, just as you like. Put in the oven and simmer till the meat can be levered fairly easily off the bones. This will take from three-quarters to an hour and a half according to age—maybe even longer for an ancient buck.

There are all sorts of trimmings and additions you can make —triangles of fried bread, fried mushrooms, crisp fried bacon, dumplings. You've already got gravy, so avoid a vegetable which has sauce over it. Peas or beans go well.

FRIED RABBIT

This method is very easy and comes in useful because the rabbit can be included as one of the ingredients of a mixed grill when there is not enough of it to go round on its own. One essential—it must be a young one, half to three-quarters grown.

Skin and joint the rabbit as before, and then simmer it in salted water for about half an hour. Take it out and let it drain and dry. Probably the best way of frying it is what the chefs call *à l'Anglais* which consists of dipping the joints in beaten-up egg and then rolling them in breadcrumbs (dried and crushed bread) before frying either in a frying pan or in deep fat. The point of this technique is that the egg-and-breadcrumb forms a more or less sealed casing around the meat, keeping the moisture in and, in effect, steaming it inside a crisp crust. If you do not want to bother with this, just put the rabbit in the frying pan along with the sausages and steak-and-kidney and fry it gently till you can get it off the bone without it flying across the kitchen.

Fried rabbit with mushrooms, tomatoes, a rasher of bacon and some chipped or *sauté* potatoes makes a very pleasant and easily-prepared meal.

RABBIT PIE

This is an excellent dish, and very well worth making. The only snag to it is that you must have some pastry; and here, I fear, I cannot help you. So far I have always been able, by the liberal use of blandishments and flattery, to get someone else to make it for me. Anyway, what better gambit could you have than "Come and make the pastry for my rabbit-pie, darling"?

Well now, presupposing that you have your glamorous pastry-maker positively champing at the bit, cook the rabbit either in the same way as for a casserole, or else dispense with the marinade and begin by flouring and frying. Then simmer in a saucepan, using cider or mild beer as a cooking liquor. Don't forget the salt. Whilst this is cooking, hard-boil three eggs and cut the rind off half a pound of bacon—smoked or plain, as you prefer. Take the meat off the bones as soon as it is ready to come. You will now have finished, for the time being, with the kitchen table; so, having fortified your pastry-maker with a couple of stiff gins, let her loose with some flour, lard, a bowl and a rolling pin. Look admiring and make encouraging noises from a safe distance.

You can either have a deep pie in the traditional pie-dish, or you can make a plate pie or pasty. The former has pastry only on top and has more gravy in it; the latter has pastry both above and below and is more solid.

For Deep Pie

Put an egg-cup in the centre of the pie-dish to support the crust if you must, but you should have sufficient filling, and arrange the boned meat, hard-boiled eggs (sliced in half, lengthways) bacon and a few mushrooms if you have them, around it. Scatter in a little thyme and freshly-ground black pepper, and fill up to the top of the meat with the cooking liquor. Hand over to your minion to have the hat put on. It will take about half an hour to cook the pastry—in a hot oven. Preferably foist this job off on to her as well, and then if it all goes up in smoke you are comparatively in the clear.

For Pasty

Use a large enamel plate for preference, but a china one will do. Line the bottom of it with pastry and pack the filling in a mound, laying the bacon strips on top so that as it melts, the fat will run into the rabbit. Put the pastry top on, cut some slits in the middle to let the steam out, and it is ready for the oven. Seasoning as for Deep Pie. If you think it will be too dry, pour about half a cup of cooking liquor in before the top goes on. Otherwise, if you are serving it hot, heat the cooking liquor up and put it on the table as gravy.

For Fricassée of Rabbit

This is merely rabbit prepared as for pie—stewed and taken off the bones. It is then cut up into unrecognisable small pieces and stirred into a white sauce with one or two chicken cubes dissolved in it. The concoction can be flavoured with anything you like—cayenne pepper, garlic, marjoram, thyme, bay leaves. Serve triangles of fried bread with it to counteract the soupiness. Not very interesting, but not much trouble and will not deteriorate with a couple of hours' delay.

* ❀ * ❀ * ❀ * ❀ * ❀ * ❀ *

PART THREE

* ❀ * ❀ * ❀ * ❀ * ❀ * ❀ *

Fish

CHAPTER VII

* ❀ *

FISH

* ❀ *

SALMON

A WARM, still evening in the middle of June. A faint on-shore breeze bringing you the smell of the sea and the distant clamour of the gulls on the sand-bar at the estuary mouth. The tide, at half flood, is coming in fast. Racing up the centre of the river with the urgency of a man going to meet his maid, it gurgles and chuckles round the weed-bearded stem and ribs of the old fishing-boat, half buried in the sand at the tide's edge. Experience gently mocking impetuosity. A mowing-machine's clatter is made drowsy by distance and the tern, fishing for sand-eels or brit in the swirling water, the most graceful sight of the day. You are still watching it—your mind miles away—when suddenly, in a flurry of green water and white foam, a yard-long bar of silver hurls itself out of the river, not ten yards hence, hangs poised for a split second and then falls back with an almighty splash. By the time you have descended once more into your gum-boots and your heart has returned to its usual position, you will have gathered that the salmon have started to run! Hundreds of miles they have come, from the perpetual starlight of the Atlantic deeps. Dodging the dolphins, circumnavigating the seals and sheering away from the sharks, they have finally reached Home—the river they were hatched in.

The biologists have discovered now that except for a very small percentage, salmon and sea-trout will always return to their native river. The "small percentage" serve a very useful purpose. They go to another river, and often another country, thereby making sure that stocks will never become inbred, and that in the unlikely eventuality of any of our rivers becoming unpolluted again, those rivers will be automatically re-stocked with salmon.

The Rules of War lay down that neither combatant shall poison the air or the water. In peace-time England one can apparently do both and get away with it. Factories belching out fumes that kill even the trees around them; great rivers turned into stinking open sewers with the chemical and animal filth constantly being tipped and pumped into them.

The love of water is a very deep and basic part of human nature. Life is literally insupportable without it; but apart from that, it has protected us from our enemies—the Channel and castle moats, for example. It provides a means of transport through otherwise impossible country and, if it is pure, contains an almost inexhaustible supply of easily caught food. And that is why (reason long ago tucked away in the subconscious, and inherent affection remaining) people will usually go somewhere near water for peace and relaxation. Fishing, sailing, boating, swimming, taking the kids to the sea-side, paddling, or just lying on the bank of the river watching the fish rising and the dragon-flies hawking gnats over the surface. But now, pathetically little is left, especially to the townsman, compared with what he should have. Cupidity, ignorance, selfishness and greed have seen to that.

Not so very long ago great runs of salmon came up all our big rivers—the Thames, Ouse, Severn, Trent, Wear and Tyne. Leaving for a moment the aesthetic viewpoint out of it, the commercial value of those fish today would be enormous; not only would a proportion be taken in stake-nets at the river mouths, but the revenue from the sale of fishing tickets on the towns' own stretch of water would be very considerable. All this, and many thousands of tons of excellent salmon, is now being lost.

Just supposing—falling over backwards to be fair—a regulation were to be brought out now which said: "If, in twenty years' time, any factory or other premises is discharging into any river or stream any liquid that the Managing Director or Owner is not prepared to drink, then that factory or premises shall be closed down until such time as the necessary alterations have been carried out".

Think of standing by Cleopatra's Needle and watching the

fun as an off-duty costermonger, cheered on by a crowd of small boys, plays and lands a twenty-pounder from the bottom of the steps. Only a dream, I suppose.

In order to understand the eatability, or even edibility, of salmon, it is necessary to know something of its life-cycle. The hen salmon lays her eggs in the autumn, in a hollow she has scooped in the gravel at the head-waters of the river, or in one of the side streams. The cock fish fertilises them in a casual sort of way, and then they are covered up again. These hatch the following spring, into an embryonic-looking little fish with a yolk-sac under it, called an alevin. Then, until it is about three inches long, it is a fry. From three to six or seven inches, it grows dark bars along its sides, and red spots like a trout. It is then a parr. After this it is growing too big for the food-supply that the river is capable of providing; so, with its contemporaries, it puts on a silver coat and goes off to the sea—as a smolt. They are then between a quarter and half a pound weight and have been in the river for three or four years. A considerable number of rivers that salmon use for spawning are what are known as "spate rivers"—in other words, mountain streams which run in a rocky, stony bed and alternate violently between a raging torrent after rain and a little trickle in fine weather. Any water plants which try to grow are promptly swept away, and consequently there is no cover or food for the larvae of the water flies and beetles on which the fish feed. Even the resident brown trout in this type of water rarely reach more than a quarter of a pound, however old they are. Besides all the foregoing disadvantages, the water coming down from the mountains, moors and peat-mosses is almost always acid, and water plants and insects like alkaline conditions.

Therefore you can take it that a spate river will not support fish that are any longer than your hand—and not so many of those, either; which brings us to the next stage.

The salmon smolt stays at sea for at least eighteen months, and usually longer, making the most of the unlimited food supply now available to it—prawns, sparling, brit, crabs, sand-eels, etc. When it returns to the river again it is called a grilse, and weighs anything from three to seven pounds. Now supposing that this fish, and hundreds more like it—some of them adults of up to fifty pounds—were to come up the river, still feeding. The result would be chaos. Everything that moved would be devoured in the first few hours, including all the fry and parr of their own species. Then, having exterminated all future generations, they would die of starvation. The fact that this is not so, and the species continues to thrive, is due to rather a remarkable dispensation of Providence.

Some weeks before the salmon reaches his river, whilst he is still coming in from the Atlantic, his digestive juices dry up and his stomach atrophies. All desire to feed is gone. The fish is in magnificent condition, and the roe (eggs in the female, milt in the male) is a mere thread, no thicker than a knitting-needle. If that fish is taken in the nets at the river mouth, or "runs" straight away and is rod-caught, it is the best salmon that you can eat. When it is cooked, it has a white curd between the flakes of fish very like the crumbly curd in a boiled egg that has been laid less than twelve hours.

From this time onwards, the fish slowly deteriorates in condition. The roe begins to develop; and the only way it can do this is to draw nourishment from the salmon's stored reserves, as no food is being eaten. The same applies to energy needed for movement and the maintenance of essential services in the salmon's body. The fish gradually loses its brilliant silver sheen, and becomes golden-coloured; then copper, and finally, by spawning time, it is blackish-grey. All this time it is getting more lank in appearance and the flesh turns from the deep red of a fresh-run fish, through pink, finally to dirty white— at which stage it is inedible and, some people maintain, actually poisonous.

After spawning, the salmon is called a kelt and, if it is accidentally caught in a river where the fresh runs are coming up as the kelts are returning to the sea, it must be released unharmed. No one but an idiot would think of doing anything else, but the fishing fraternity in common with most others, has its fair share!

Smoked salmon is a commodity which lends itself to a lot of

chicanery by unscrupulous merchants, caterers and hoteliers. How often have you heard "No thank you, I won't have any smoked salmon; I don't understand what people see in it"? Or even, "Filthy stuff. I wouldn't feed it to my cat!" You have probably come across the rubbish in question yourself. The same colour and appearance as pink blotting-paper or flannel. This is not smoked salmon; it is smoked kelt—or as near kelt as makes no difference. And I suspect that some of it is dyed with cochineal. There is a story which I wish I could vouch for, about a couple of early teen-age kids whose parents were giving a cocktail party. One of the main "snacks" (horrible word) was little squares of smoked salmon on brown bread and butter. It must have been the kind that we are talking about, because the temptation to replace it with squares of pink lint, or some other material of the correct appearance, proved too strong for the little pets. I must admit I would dearly have loved to watch the guests' efforts, first to eat it, and then to ditch it somewhere without being spotted.

Smoked salmon should be a fish taken early in the season, and sent straight to the curers. The Jews do some of the best work; there is an excellent firm on the edge of Soho. When you get your side back (leave the other side in cold store, with the curers, till you need it) and cut into it, the flesh should be slightly transparent, dark red, and oily. Furthermore, it should have an exceedingly appetising smell. The other stuff smells like the day after the fire on the fish-dock.

Smoked salmon is carved with a long, very sharp knife. A worn, old carving-knife is ideal, as it is also slightly flexible. I don't suppose it matters much which end you start at, but the shoulder is the more usual. Carve with a very long sloping cut, taking the slices off as thinly as you can—aim at wafers. On an average side, the distance from the beginning of the cut, at the top, to where it ends up on the skin, should be at least four inches—preferably more. It is exceedingly irritating to have to watch some berk hacking the stuff off in thick chunks, cut straight down, even if he *has* paid for it! It doesn't taste the same somehow. All you need now is some fresh brown bread and butter, a pepper mill with black pepper-corns in it, and a reasonably ripe lemon—cut in half. I'll swop you my caviare for your salmon any day!

Most other fish are very much better eaten hot rather than cold. Salmon is an exception and is, if anything, nicer cold. I have found that the best way of dealing with a salmon, or a big sea-trout, is to cut it in two, just behind the dorsal fin, using the tail end to eat hot, as steaks, and the front piece to boil or bake, and allow to get cold.

SALMON STEAKS

Take the tail piece of the fish and cut it into slices—straight through—with a large, heavy knife. Somewhere between an inch and an inch-and-a-half thickness will ensure that the middle is properly cooked by the time that the outside looks as if it has had enough. Beat up an egg on a plate, dip the steaks in it, and then roll them in breadcrumbs. Fry in a butter/olive oil mixture, and fry slowly. Turn the heat down until the steaks are sizzling gently. All you will achieve with quick-frying will be a burnt outside and raw middle. Cook for about six or seven minutes on each side. A very useful indication, when frying a thick piece of food which you want cooked right through (as opposed to the surface-blasting that a beefsteak needs) is that when the article has been cooking for some time on its second side, listen for a sudden crescendo of bubbling and spitting from the frying-pan. This means that the cookery from the second side has met up in the middle with that from the first side. At this point it appears that the juices in the food are released, and begin to run out into the boiling fat—hence the noise. Take whatever it is out at once, and it should be just right.

It will only be practical to take off steaks to within about seven or eight inches of the tail, so fry the end piece intact—having, of course, cut away the actual tail fin.

To eat with your salmon steaks, I would suggest new potatoes and peas; or, if later in the year, boiled rice and scarlet runner beans. You would probably like some sauce too; and so this seems as good a time as any to give you the other two traditional

sauces—Béchamel and Hollandaise. The third, Espagnole, is
included in the chapter on Mutton.

Béchamel Sauce

This is the basis of all the main white sauces used with fish,
white meats, vegetables and eggs. It is really not so very much
more trouble to make than the ordinary "butter, flour and
milk" white sauce, and well worth it if you want to do a bit of
showing off!

Collect up some butter, onion, carrot, celery, flour, milk,
peppercorns, bay leaf, mushroom stalks, thyme, nutmeg and
salt. Chop finely one small onion, one carrot, a stick of celery,
and the mushroom stalks. Put an ounce of butter in a heavy
saucepan and heat to just below the boil. Tip the chopped
vegetables in, and let them cook very slowly, without colouring,
for about ten minutes. Scoop out the vegetables and put them
on one side; add another ounce of butter and allow it to melt.
Scatter in about a tablespoon of flour—more or less—so that
the butter and the flour combine to form a *roux* which is neither
too crumbly nor too sloppy. Stir and cook this roux slowly,
without letting it colour, and thus spoil the whiteness of your
sauce, for two or three minutes. Now start adding a pint of
milk—a little at a time, and stirring hard the while to avoid
lumps. Bring to the boil (more stirring), by which time it ought
to be the consistency of a thinnish cream.

Return the vegetables to the pan and add a pinch of thyme,
a bay leaf, twelve peppercorns, a grating of nutmeg and a
suitable amount of salt. Simmer very slowly for about an hour
with the pan uncovered, stirring now and again. Finally tip
the lot into a big, round-bottomed strainer and press the liquid
through with a spoon—but don't be so energetic that you sieve
the vegetables through as well. If you think your sauce is too
thin, just boil it down (more stirring) until it is the consistency
you want.

Having made this sauce, the field is wide open to you. You
can have Shrimp sauce, Parsley sauce, Egg sauce or any other
sauce you like, by the simple expedient of chopping up shrimps,

parsley or eggs (hard-boiled—need I add!) etc., and stirring them.

Hollandaise Sauce

This has been on the go in the kitchens of the High and Mighty since the early seventeen hundreds. It is an entirely different type from the other two, being thickened with yolk of egg instead of flour—in fact, it is really a kind of hot mayonnaise. Because of the egg yolk thickening, it must be cooked in a *bain-marie*—which is nothing more or less than a basin standing in boilng water, or in a double pan.

Equip yourself with half a port glass of white wine, one port glass of water, a quarter pound of butter, two egg yolks, salt and pepper, and half a lemon.

Put the wine and water together in a saucepan and boil them till you only have half a glass of port left. Tip this into the *bain-marie*. Beat the egg yolks and stir them into the wine/water. Now add the butter, in small pieces, stirring all the time till you have got rid of it, and the sauce has thickened. Season carefully, and finally add some lemon juice.

This sauce is sometimes used with asparagus, but is more usually served with such fish as salmon, Dover sole, brill and sea-trout.

Boiled Rice

There are various methods of cooking rice for eating with fish, curries, Chinese food, etc.—some more involved than others; but the one I use I learnt from an old sea-captain whom I met in a prison camp in Poland. An inspiring character he was, even under those conditions. His salt-bleached blue eyes glittered and his iron-grey beard bristled with fury whenever he allowed himself to think about the German nation. He used to tell us stories of the days when he was serving his apprenticeship in square-rig, of the Kaiser's War, and all kinds of capers he had been mixed up in whilst we were kicking in our cradles—if we'd even got as far as that! Now the Skipper, as we somewhat disrespectfully called him, was uncommonly fond of curry, and the next best thing to eating it was to tell us how it ought to be made—and, in particular, how the rice should be cooked. "You must have Patna rice" he would say. "Put it into a pan of boiling water, with salt in, and boil it for TWELVE MINUTES." He would sometimes pound on the table with a great fist like a ham, making our precious pot mugs leap in the air. "Not eleven-and-a-half minutes and not twelve and a half minutes, but TWELVE MINUTES" he roared, in a voice that would blast through a sou'westerly gale like a charge of buckshot and, I should think, send the very fish scurrying to the bottom for shelter! "Then you strain off the boiling water and wash the rice under the cold tap. This both cleans the stickiness away and stops the cooking immediately. When you want to use it, pour more boiling water on to it, bring almost to the boil, strain again thoroughly, and whack it out. It saves all the faffing about, drying trays of rice in the oven."

Having disposed of the after-end of the salmon, we'd better return and deal with the for'ard half. As a salmon does not feed, there is no need for it to be gutted with the same speed and thoroughness as there is for other fish. It is by no means uncommon for it to be hung (ungutted) in the same way as game. The flavour is said to improve; but somehow I still think I'd rather eat mine as fresh as possible.

Take the head off the piece—there is no point in leaving it on, it only takes up more room—and clean out the abdominal cavity, or tunnel, without slitting it open if possible. If the piece of fish is left "round" it looks better, and also holds together better when lifting it out of the fish kettle.

As you are unlikely to have a special fish-kettle, the only thing you will have that is big enough to take half a salmon will be the larger roasting tin. An heirloom that I acquired from the attic of an aunt's house some years ago has been very useful. It is an oval, flat, china plate roughly 14″ × 10″ willow pattern, and with holes of an eighth-inch scattered around a larger one in the centre. There is a rim of perhaps a quarter-inch round the edge, on the under side. It has been useful to me for cooking large pieces of fish. I put it in the bottom of the roasting tin—having first of all threaded two bits of wire through the holes at each end, thereby making handles to lift it by—and put the fish on it. Or rather, put the fish on it first, and then lower it into the boiling salt and water in the tin.

It is very easy to put a lump of salmon in a vessel and cook it; but it is a horse of a different colour when the time comes to get it out again without breaking it up. And so, although you may not be able to lay your hands on an exactly identical article—a junk shop would be the place to look—I would rig up some similar contraption, if you think you will be doing enough of this cooking to make it worthwhile.

However, presupposing that you have the roasting-tin half full of boiling salted water, lower the salmon into it and, when the water tries to return to the boil, reduce heat until it is just moving—swirling gently—around the fish. Poaching, in other words. Give it ten minutes to the pound, then turn off the heat and allow the fish to cool in the cooking liquor. The idea of doing this is to keep the fish moist; if it is taken out of boiling water and allowed to steam itself dry and cold, the tendency will be for the texture to become rather fibrous. Put it on a plate somewhere cool, and out of the way of the cat and the bluebottles.

You are now drawing very close to another of those hurdles which clutter up one's path through life:

Salad! You may, in your innocence, imagine that you merely have to gather a lettuce, some tomatoes, radishes, chives, cucumber, and hard-boiled egg; chop them all up, pour a mixture of olive oil, vinegar and sugar over the lot, stir it up, and—lo and behold—you have a salad. I think so too, but we would both be wrong. The distaff side would dismiss our efforts as a scruffy compost-heap. However, do not despair, and I will shortly tell you how you can turn an odd fixation in the feminine make-up to your own advantage—with a little bit of luck! Nearly all girls (from nineteen to ninety) have a secret conviction that nobody but themselves is really fit to be trusted to make pastry, make salads, or look after a baby. The last fallacy is immediately explodable—any idiot can look after a baby; otherwise the human race would have come to a grinding stop hundreds of thousands of years ago! On short reflection, that doesn't seem such a bad idea either.

This leaves us with pastry and salads. Pastry has already been dealt with in earlier chapters by your old friend Flakey Flossie. But pastry, and Flossie, are winter dishes. When the hot summer breeze wafts the scent of June roses through the window and the swallows skim low over the lawn as they hunt flies to feed their nestlings up in the corner of your porch, you may begin to feel that you have had a surfeit of pastry, for the time being anyway, and a change of diet would not come amiss. This, Gentle Reader, is the moment to reach for the phone and see whether Luscious Lettie, the Salad Queen, is at home! "Lettie darling, *do* come over. I've got a cucumber and some tomatoes, and all sorts of things. You're *so* much better at dealing with them than I am." If she hesitates at all, add quickly "I've just bought a bottle of gin"—which should clinch matters.

It is usually better if she is not a chum of Flossie's—otherwise you may come unstuck. By the way, if you keep hens, you will find they are very good at eating up all those stale lettuces and mouldy tomatoes that never got used!

SEA-TROUT

These fish have very much the same life-cycle as the salmon, but are literally a seagoing brown trout being, as I understand, indistinguishable from an anatomical point of view. The first-year fish, corresponding to the salmon grilse, is called a herling or, in the north-west of England, a smelt. The adult sea-trout is locally called a morgt. This is apparently the ancient Norse word for much, or big; so presumably smelt means little, or small. Whereas the salmon goes away into the Atlantic during his sea trips, the sea-trout is thought to remain near the mouth of his own river, until the time comes for him to come up again to spawn.

From the culinary point of view, there is no difference in the treatment of a large sea-trout and a salmon; but the herling, which weigh anything from a quarter of a pound to a pound, are at their best when fried with bacon, for breakfast. You just slit them open for the entire length of the belly, take out the guts and scrape out the stuff that looks like congealed blood, lying along the underside of the backbone. Push it out with your thumb nail. Then cut off the head and tail, wash, and fry in shallow fat for five to eight minutes a side, according to size. Serve with bacon and fried bread, and you have a breakfast fit for a king.

Another good breakfast or supper dish which uses up the rest of the cold boiled salmon when you can no longer face it, is a cross between kedgeree and fish-cake—made like this:

SALMON CAKES

Take the salmon off the bones, and break it up into small pieces. Add to it the same volume of boiled Patna rice—you probably have some left over, already cooked—two or three hard-boiled eggs chopped up, and a generous ration of chopped parsley; black pepper and salt. Mix it all up in a bowl and stick it together with raw egg until it can be made into cakes that won't fall apart too easily. Coat with beaten egg and bread-crumbs and fry till golden. Bacon and fried bread again.

BROWN TROUT

This can be an excellent fish to eat, or it can be very dis-appointing and muddy. This variation, as with wildfowl, etc., is explained by the food that the creature lives on. It is a seeming paradox that trout from a clear mountain stream taste muddy, whilst those from a comparatively muddy chalky stream are as good as any you will find. The reason that this is often so, lies in the fact that the alkaline water of the latter provides the conditions that water plants and insects thrive on. Therefore the trout have an abundant food supply which they take from the surface of the water—ephemera, sedges, stone-flies and beetles—and also freshwater shrimps and snails in mid-water. They consequently grow fast and never have to grub around on the bottom for any old rubbish they can find to keep them-selves alive—like those in the crystal clear pools have to. They, poor fish, have their work cut out to keep body and soul together—let alone provide an epicure's guzzle!

Brown Trout, which includes Loch Leven and Rainbow Trout, are usually fried in butter or, alternatively, casseroled in white wine, butter and parsley. Gut the fish in the same way as for herling and, if they are small enough to fit in your frying-pan with their heads and tails left on, leave them on. Fry very slowly, so that the skin does not burn on to the flesh. When you come to think of it, a fish fried slowly in its skin is really not being fried at all, but steamed—or literally "stewed in its own juice". To cook the trout in wine, you make a mixture of white wine, melted butter, and chopped parsley in an oval pot casserole, with a lid. Bring to the boil in the oven, lay the trout in, cover, and simmer for about ten minutes. Turn the fish and cook for another five minutes. If you are going to eat them cold, leave them to cool in the cooking liquor.

Everything except salmon, sea-trout and trout—which are called Game Fish—that lives in fresh water in the British Isles, is classed as a Coarse Fish. From a culinary viewpoint, at any rate, this is by no means a bad description. Were I a medieval monk, faced with the alternative diets of Fresh Air and Scourge or Boiled Carp, I would take the carp—but only just!

The only coarse fish that I have eaten and really enjoyed, is perch. These particular ones came out of a mountain tarn, and so would taste considerably better than if they had come out of a canal. I gutted them and skinned them, then they were left overnight in salt and water. Fried, with bacon, for breakfast, they were excellent.

Pike, so I am told, can make quite a pleasant meal. I have only eaten it once, myself, and was not particularly impressed; but that may easily have been the fault of the preparation and/ or cooking. It seems that the best way of going about it is this: Start with a fish of around seven pounds—the smaller, or Jack pike are very bony, and the larger ones rather coarse—gut it and leave it in salt water for twelve hours; then dry it and fill the abdominal cavity with forcemeat stuffing. Stitch up with needle and cotton. Spread with butter, wrap in tinfoil, and bake in the oven for about three-quarters of an hour, according to the heat available. Apparently it then becomes quite edible gear!

In the Daffodil Days, before Hitler and his thugs marched into the Rhineland, I, as a very young subaltern, was in Company camp beside a little river on the borders of Norfolk and Suffolk. On these expeditions I always carried an eight-foot dry fly rod with me, as part of my normal military equipment; and so, when I was not slogging either to or fro' the Ranges, or engaged in some other Duties of National Importance, I would go and flick a fly over the fish I could see rising in the pool below the camp. Slender, silvery little fish, with red fins. Having done all my fishing in the Northern counties, where there are very few coarse fish, I didn't know what they were until someone told me they were dace. They were very small, and I used to put them back again; until one day I caught a monster fish—it must have been every ounce of half-a-pound—which I thought would make me a splendid breakfast. It was different from the dace. A very deep, but comparatively narrow fish, covered with large silver scales. My batman, who was a local lad, said it was a roach; I thought he gave me rather an old-fashioned look when I asked him if he would cook it for my breakfast—but he just said, "Very good, Sir" and went off with it. When it appeared on my plate the next morning, it looked marvellous—fried to perfection. "Cotton wool and pins" would not be a truly accurate description; perhaps, if you can imagine trying to eat wet shoddy with nylon tooth-brush bristles mixed liberally into it, you will be getting close to the texture. The flavour was reminiscent of stirred-up horse-pond after a prolonged period of drought. The grinning face of Ling appeared round the tent flap. "Enjoying your breakfast, Sir?" he asked, and hurriedly vanished.

And so I would be inclined to leave all the chub, bream, carp, tench, roach, rudd and dace to the herons and pike. They bolt their fish whole and so are not bothered by bones!

A Victorian jaunt, which must have been quite fun—in the right company—was a Gudgeon Party. The young men and maidens of the house-party, attired in suitably frivolous manner, climbed into carriages, traps, dog-carts, or whatever they could winkle out of Papa, and headed for the Thames. They were followed, at a discreet distance, by James, the under-footman, and one of the maids, in the Shopping Equipage. On arrival, they hired punts from some low fellow who had punts for hire. Furious activity—putting up fishing-rods, sorting out tackle, arranging cushions, etc. followed. In the middle of it all some unspeakable bounder and utter cad dropped a worm down Miss Ethel's neck. Finally the fishing fleet put to sea and the serious business of catching gudgeon began. Gudgeon are little fish, only a few inches long, which must have abounded in the Thames around that time—and indeed may still do so, for all I know. They are very easily caught, and after an hour or two, during which George diverted the company by falling in for the second time, enough had been taken.

James and the girl had, meanwhile, unpacked the picnic hampers, got a little fire going, and a frying-pan at the ready. The party poled ashore and sat around on the grassy bank, engaging each other in witty, but decorous, conversation; James, meanwhile, was frying up the gudgeon—in the same way as one would cook sprats—and Susan spreading the bread and butter. After tea, followed by a jolly game of Hide-and-Seek in the bushes—which was all George had come for anyway—the company set out for home, in time to dress before dinner, and prepared themselves for any further debaucheries the evening might have in store.

EEL is, I think, the only fish of importance not yet mentioned. A fair-sized eel (two feet and upwards) is a very high-quality fish; I can't be bothered with the little ones—Devil's Bootlaces, my old Guv'nor used to call them. There are fried eels, jellied eels, stewed eels, elver cake, etc., but the one that beats the lot, as far as I am concerned, is the smoked eel that comes (I think) from Holland. You don't often come across it except in plushy London restaurants—but if you do, I strongly advise you to whack in, and without further delay!

If you have a big eel that you want to cook yourself, you go about it like this: Get a piece of strong string, about two feet long, and tie the ends together. Pass the knot through the loop at the other end, so as to form a noose. Put this noose round the eel's neck, just below the head, pull tight, and hang the eel up on a strong nail. With a sharp knife, cut round the skin just below the string; now take hold of the edge of this skin with a pair of pliers. A strong, long tug downwards will remove the skin entirely—inside out. Cut off the head, clean out the guts, and chop into three-inch lengths.

An eel is inclined to be an oily fish and so is specially suitable to be cooked in a dry white wine—such as white Beaujolais; this will take off the oiliness and bring out the flavour. Fry the chunks lightly and slowly in butter—so that the butter does not become discoloured—place them in a covered pot casserole of the right size; pour the butter over them and then cover with wine. Add pepper and salt—with a touch of garlic too, if you like it. Simmer in the oven. Half an hour should be plenty.

So far, I have dealt only with fresh-water fish—which, I suppose, are more a countryman's province than those in the sea. But, as sea fish are nearly always of a far higher quality, a selection of them must be included. I will suppose that you are a fisherman, and that you live within reach of the sea—or, better still, an unpolluted estuary—and start with the things you are likely to catch and find there.

BASS

Bass is probably the most exciting fish you will encounter, either in the estuary or fishing from the shore. And, furthermore, probably the best to eat. The bass is a salt-water perch, and is sometimes called Sea-bass, to differentiate between it and the fresh-water perch—which is also called a bass in some localities. In spite of its large head, compared with a salmon or sea-trout, it is a magnificent fish to look at. Silver flanks, and an olive green back; it has a ferocious dorsal fin, with spikes like darning-needles along the top of it. The gill-covers are sharp, and will cut your hand if you are not careful. In size, it runs from half-a-pound for school-bass—or those which go about together in a shoal—up to twelve pounds and over for the fish you dream of, as you cast your spoon across the flood tide in the estuary, or loaf in a boat on a hot summer's afternoon—probably lying in a backwater in the lower reaches of a Devonshire river—watching a big float which has a treble hook and a couple of live prawns dangling below it. At any moment it may disappear with a "plop" as that enormous bass grabs the bait!

After a Homeric battle, during which your line was run out to the last few yards of backing, and your rod creaked as you risked everything by braking the reel hard, the Bass of the Year rolls on his side and floats gently in over a net that usually looks quite inadequate to deal with it. The gods are on your side for once, and he's in the boat. By the time you have called in at every pub on the way home to show him off to your chums, you'll be so glassy-eyed that it will be a job to tell the difference between you and the bass!

I have found that the best way of cooking a large bass is to daub it with butter, wrap it in tin-foil, and bake it in the oven—having, of course, cleaned it and taken the head off first. The flesh is white, and of a very good flavour. Small fish, of between half-a-pound and a pound, are best fried in the same way as herling.

FLOUNDERS OR FLUKES

Flounders or Flukes are another estuary fish which provides both an hour or two's entertainment and a good supper. Fluke-spearing is not as easy as it looks. The equipment needed is simple, consisting of a pair of sea-boots, a bag to put the fish in, and a spear with anything from one to four tines—not, as a rule, barbed. A pitchfork will do at a pinch. The technique is to wait till the tide is out, and only fresh water is running through the river bed; then wade upstream; prodding with the spear in all the likely places that a fluke might be lying buried in the sand—behind rocks, under streamers of seaweed, etc. A jiggling of the spear will tell you when you have got one. Bend down and take a firm hold of the fish before you withdraw the prong that is holding it. A barbed spear makes such a mess of the fluke when it is pulled out that, as I said, it is not generally used.

Except to feed the cat, I would not bother to spear flukes in estuary mud that is never covered by fresh water. Any that I have ever tried to eat, caught in such a place, have been most unpleasant. Those speared in sand, with fresh water running over them, are excellent.

To prepare these fish, cut off the head and tail, and clean out the guts. Beware of a very sharp bone which sticks forward just below the pectoral fin; it can give you a nasty jab and is inclined to be poisonous. Wash the fish, dry them, dust with flour, and shallow-fry them. Only a few minutes on each side for the little ones, and seven to eight for the big ones. Pile the flukes on a plate, and put them on the table with a new brown loaf, a large pat of butter, a plate for wreckage, and mugs of strong tea all round. Preferably eat them the same day as they are caught.

SAND DABS

Of all the flat-fish these are probably the finest-flavoured. They are caught outside the estuary, on the sandy bottom of the shore and, fishing from a boat, you can sometimes pull them up as fast as you can re-bait and lower your line again. Usually not much bigger than your hand, they are the colour of the sand on which they live. Preparation, cooking and eating is exactly the same as for flukes.

LOBSTER

A few years after the war I was staying in South Devon with an old Air Force friend—a very experienced sailor and fisherman. At this time he owned a large Newlyn lugger, the *Veracity*, and had her fitted out as a trawler. It was a hot summer's afternoon; the trawl had been shot, and we were sitting on deck, smoking and talking of this and that. I said, "Do you ever get any lobsters in the trawl?" He looked at me pityingly. "My dear fellow, you find lobsters amongst rocks, and we're halfway across Tor Bay—in the middle of a square mile of sand." "Oh", said I, with due humility. After another half-hour or so, the trawl was hauled. I can see it now, as it came in with the water streaming off it. There was nothing in it—no fish, no seaweed, no crabs, no starfish—except one enormous lobster. Six pounds, I seem to remember. My old chum's face was, as they say, A Study. I, excusably I think, fell about!

Lobsters are normally caught in baited wickerwork pots, which are set in deep water, on a reef of rocks. It is no use trying it on a shallow shore (as I did once) because the sea will pound the pots to bits, and/or ravel the rope carrying the marker float, in the weed. The marker doesn't surface, and you lose the lot. In some places there is a reef of lobstery rocks which is uncovered on a low spring tide. Then you can go, with a crab-hook, and help yourself. Be careful when you pick a lobster up; if it gets you with its pincers you will know all about it; and if it shuts its tail on your fingers you will have a very nasty injury. Pick it up just behind the point where the claws join the body—fingers on one side of the shell, thumb on the other. It will swing its great gnashers back to try and get you, but can't quite reach—and you are safe from the tail. Tie the claws up with string (get someone to hold one claw whilst you tie the other) or the lobsters will tear each other to bits in the bag.

There are, of course, many ways of cooking lobster. Some of them so highly seasoned that the true flavour is lost. Unless one has so many lobsters that new ways of cooking them have to be found to relieve the monotony—which is unlikely—I can recommend the following technique:

Suppose you have caught one of about two pounds—there he is, all alive-o, and looking very sinister in his dark blue armour plating. Put on to boil some large container with salted water in it. I use a bucket on a Primus stove. When the water boils, drop the lobster in, headfirst, and move back quickly, because sometimes his tail will flip and splash you with hot water. The sudden shock of the boiling water seems to knock the lobster unconscious almost immediately. You can dismiss the story you may hear, that a lobster sometimes screams when it is dropped in. The "scream" is simply air, expanded by the heat, forcing its way out through joints in the shell. Anyway, a lobster has no vocal chords! Boil a two-pounder for about twenty minutes, a much larger one for half-an-hour, and a smaller one for only a quarter. As the lobster cooks, it is interesting to watch the colour change from blue/black to coral red.

When the lobster is cooked, put it in the larder to cool. This, of course, would seem a good time to ring up Luscious Lettie and ask her if she would like to trade a Salad Session for a bit of lobster! In the interval before she arrives, you may as well get on with your half of the bargain. Put the lobster on the kitchen table, right side up, and with its tail spread out. Take a short, heavy, sharp knife (a skinning knife is ideal) and, being careful not to slip and gash yourself, cut it in half, lengthways. The knife will shear through the shell quite easily if enough pressure is put on it. Replace in the larder.

You will enjoy eating lobster more if you depart from the usually accepted rules of etiquette. For a start, cover the dining table with sheets of newspaper; then go and find two flat stones, about a foot square, and scrub them clean. Go to the workshop and fetch a couple of hammers, and scrub them too. Now you can lay the table. Knife and fork with, on the left, a bread-and-butter plate and, on the right, a flat stone and hammer! A new loaf of brown bread, lots of butter, salt and pepper. The rest is up to Lettie—if she ever gets around to it. If you haven't got a lobster pick (and not many people have), a fine-tined carving fork is quite a useful tool. When you come to square up afterwards, you will see the wisdom of the newspapers on the table. The place looks like Hampstead Heath on Bank Holiday Tuesday!

CRABS

Crabs seem to be found more on the north-east coast of England than the north-west; therefore I have had little experience of them. At some periods of the year there is hardly anything to eat in them, and so they are not worth buying.

They seem to be in very good condition in October—I associate, in my mind, the eating of crabs and the conkers falling from the horse-chestnut trees. Whereas you can eat all of a lobster, you must take the "Dead men's fingers" out of a crab; they are said to be poisonous.

As far as I remember, a crab is boiled in the same way as a lobster. To dress it, you lay it on its back and open it like a box. Inside you will see some rather unpleasant looking grey/green things, which might (with a considerable stretching of the imagination) look something like dead men's fingers. Fish them out and throw them away. Now you can get on with the tedious business of picking all the meat out of the shell and claws—the legs too, if the crab is a real Granfer. The proper cookery books will tell you all about the weird and wonderful bodge-ups you can make with the result of your labours. Me—I'd send for Lettie!

CODLING

As these fish come close inshore during the winter months, they can be caught either by surf-casting from the shore with a short powerful rod and a heavy lead; or on long-lines set over the rocks and along the sand at low tide. These lines usually have about a hundred hooks on them, baited with lug-worm, sand eel, soft crabs, bits of herring or mackerel, or anything else you can lay your hands on in sufficient quantity. Seagulls are the main snag to this caper. You have to cover your bait with little piles of sand as you set your line, to prevent them from guzzling the lug-worms, etc.; and you have to follow the tide out (by day) so that you will get the fish before they do! You will also get the occasional plaice, turbot and bass on the line too, as well as codling. If one day you find hooks torn off, worse still, the whole issue gone, you can take your choice in handing out the blame among dogfish, tope, big skate or conger eel. They are all capable of wrecking a long-line.

The words "Boiled Cod" always conjure up two pictures in my mind. The first is of the plates of slimy, malodorous muck

"It's good for you; eat it up" that I was sometimes given as a child. The second is a much happier memory. In May or June of 1941 I was stationed on a Bomber aerodrome in North-East Scotland. Recently a decision had been taken to allow the W.A.A.F.'s to be Mess Waitresses. Dixie Dean, my co-pilot, and I had just landed. After the usual formalities, we walked up to the Mess, had an abstemious half-pint apiece, and went in to lunch. We had disposed of our dollop of Brown Windsor —in long-suffering silence—and the next course arrived. The plates contained two lumps of different substances—the larger lump was white and smelt like a dirty fish-box; the smaller lump was a brownish khaki colour and looked rather rude.

"Just a minute," said Dixie.

"Yes, Sir."

"What's this?"

"Stuffed cod, Sir." He gazed at his plate for a few more seconds and then swung round and looked up at her with a beaming smile that must have made her heart flutter.

"Will you do something for me, my dear?"

"Of course, Sir."

"Take this horrible fish back to the cook, give him my compliments, and tell him to stuff it again—and make a proper job this time." The girl's eyes were twinkling, and the corners of her mouth twitching. She didn't trust herself to speak, but took the plate and almost ran across the dining-room, her shoulders shaking. She just managed to get round the screen before she exploded into peals of mirth. We heard chortles and giggles fading into the nether regions. What we didn't know was that cook was not an R.A.F. chef, but an exceedingly unpopular Sergeant W.A.A.F.!

Our Waaflet must have made the most of her message because, for the next fortnight, whenever she saw Dixie she burst out laughing again.

Codling, on the other hand, is literally a very different kettle of fish. If you can catch one of between four and six pounds, or buy one newly landed from an inshore trawler, you will have a fish that even Escoffier (bow, please!) speaks of with something approaching enthusiasm. Olive-green and white, with the

sea-sparkle still on it, the eye still looking alive. Poles apart
from the flabby, grey, hold-stinking corpses disgorged by boats
from the far-off fishing grounds.

If the fish is from a trawler, it will already be gutted, but if
you have caught it yourself, gut it as soon as possible. Now to
fillet it: use a large sharp knife, lay the fish on its side and make
a cut, straight down, directly behind the gill-cover. Angle the
cut slightly, so that you will not waste the meat at the back of
the head. Then, with the flat of the knife parallel to the table,
cut down the upper side of the backbone, from the back of the
head to the tail. Don't shear through the rib bones, but work
the knife over them. Cut gently. through till you have one
fillet clear. Turn the fish over and repeat the process on the
other side. Alternatively, get your local fishmonger to demon-
strate.

In all cod and haddock fillets there is a line of little bones
which come out from the backbone, just above the ribs.
Cutting through these is unavoidable, but they should be
picked out before the fish is cooked.

I don't think there is any better way of cooking codling than
frying it. Pour a little milk into a plate and scatter some dried
breadcrumbs on to a newspaper. Dip the fillets in the milk and
then roll them in the breadcrumbs. Put a lump of lard, or a
splash of pea-nut oil, in your biggest frying pan and bring it to
the boil—that is, when a thin blue vapour can just be seen
rising from the pan. Put the fillets in with the skin side uppermost, to begin with. Watch very carefully that the pan does
not get too hot and starts to burn the breadcrumbs, or the
flavour of your fish will be spoiled. Keep shaking the pan for
some time after the fillets are put in, to prevent them sticking
to the bottom. I do not understand this sticking business. Sometimes you can fry fillets of fish with no trouble at all; another
time, you do exactly the same thing and the fish seems to
exude some kind of glue which attaches itself firmly to the
bottom of the frying-pan and resists all efforts to get the fish
off in one piece. By the time you've chiselled it out and on to
a plate, it looks like the dog's dinner. Rather than admit
defeat, I would suggest that you take the fish off what is left

of the skin, pile it neatly in the middle of the plate, sprinkle it with paprika and chopped parsley, and serve it amid vague mutterings:

"Special way of cooking fish that I learnt from a Bulgar I met in Mombasa—nice chap he was; wore half a moustache and a gold ring in the opposite ear. They like their food a bit greasy out there!!" Provided your guests don't know you too well, you'll probably get away with it!

Supposing that these fillets are behaving themselves as they ought—turn them over after about a couple of minutes; by this time the crumbs should be a golden/brown colour. Reduce heat, and finish cooking with the skin side down. Another five minutes or so, according to the thickness of the piece. I have noticed that fish and egg seem to take about the same time to cook. For instance, frying an egg and frying a fillet of plaice of the same thickness.

Have a folded piece of newspaper in a warm oven, ready to put the fish on when you take it out of the pan. This will absorb any surplus grease. A quartered lemon, on the table, is a help, as also is some egg sauce. Serve with chipped potatoes, boiled rice, or bread-and-butter—according, as they say, to "availability of time and materials!"

The larger flat-fish—plaice, turbot, brill and small halibut—are always bought ready filleted. Cook them in the same way as the codling; or, for a change, roll the fillets up and cook them in a casserole with white wine, butter and parsley.

Before leaving the subject of white fish, I will give you an original (as far as I know) recipe for a dish that has somehow acquired the rather inelegant name of "Fish Splodge!"

Collect up: 1½ to 2-lbs. fresh filleted haddock
½-lb. mushrooms
1-lb. (or ½-kilo) tin of Italian tomatoes
4 eggs
¼-lb. Parmesan cheese
Butter, flour and milk—for white sauce.

Take the bones out of the haddock, milk-and-breadcrumb it, and fry it. Take the fish off the skin—put the former on one side; give the latter to the dog. Hardboil the eggs, shell them, and quarter them. By the way, if, after hardboiling eggs, you put them straight away under the cold tap, and keep them there for a few minutes, you will find that they will peel very much more easily.

If the mushrooms are small ones, you only need to slice them straight down through the middle, stalk and all; but if they are big ones, cut in quarters and chop the stem fairly finely.

Grate, or slice, the Parmesan cheese. Open the tomato can. Now make an ordinary white sauce—a lump of butter about an inch-and-a-half cube, melted in a heavy saucepan, with flour stirred into it till a *roux* has been made. Pour the milk in a bit at a time, stirring off the fire for a short time after each new lot of milk, until the sauce is fairly thick. Put plenty of black pepper and salt in, and then add the cheese and cook and stir until it has all melted.

In a large glass casserole, put layers of fish, mushroom, egg and tomato, till all your material has been used up; then pour the sauce over the lot, and put it in the oven. Everything in the dish, with the exception of the mushrooms, is already cooked, and so all you need do is to bring it to the boil. The point in having a glass cooking vessel is that you can see what is going on, without having to take it out of the oven.

Serve with triangles of fried bread, so that you will get a crouton effect to contrast with the softness of the Splodge.

HERRING

Of all the fish in the sea, the herring is probably the most important. Its nickname "The Pig of the Sea" indicates that its uses are as numerous as those of its grunting, earth-bound counterpart. Fresh herring, kippers, Bismarck herring, bloaters, roll-mops, smokies, red herring, pickled (or soused) herring— and probably many more that I have never heard of.

I wonder if the Northumbrian fisher-girls still go round in their traditional costume—a long, full-skirted navy blue serge dress, with many capes over the shoulders—a great creel of herring slung on their backs, crying "Calla hairn! Calla hairn!" ("Fresh herring") as they sell the catch from door to door. I shouldn't think so; it must have been a back-breaking, heart-breaking job. The picturesque aspect would be little consolation for blistered feet and a half-dislocated shoulder!

I will only give you two recipes for cooking herring; one to be eaten hot and the other cold.

The first essential, when eating herring, is to buy it at the right time—when it is at its best. This is usually in the summer —June or July—when the roe has started to develop, but not gone too far. The test is easy; if you can bone it without any of the bones breaking off, it is good. If you can't, it's not!

Filleted herring is very simple. Cut through the backbone just behind the head, with a knife. Pull the head off, and the guts will come away with it. Hold the fish in your left hand, head end towards you, and open up the belly with your right thumb. When you come to the end of the ribs, push your thumb into the fish, so that it rests on the backbone. Continue down to the tail, ploughing the fish open with the side of the thumb. Turn it round and, holding it in the other hand, and using the left thumb, clear the backbone up to the head end. Now you have the fish spread out flat, with the spine adhering to one side. Slip a knife between the spine and the flesh, immediately above the tail, and cut the tail clear. Holding the tail fin between the thumb and forefinger of the right hand, and pressing the flesh under it to the table with the fingers of the left hand, peel the backbone upwards and away from you. It should come out with all the small bones still attached to it. Rinse the herring in cold water, and stack them up to drain.

HERRING FRIED IN OATMEAL

This is, not surprisingly, a Scots dish. If you are just about broke and you suddenly discover that a great horde of ravenous relations—kids and all—is about to descend on you for lunch— THIS is the thing to feed 'em on! All you do is to roll the filleted herrings in coarse oatmeal (having dipped them in milk first) and then fry them till the oatmeal goes golden. The secret of their success (as the wily Scotch discovered!) is that the oatmeal rapidly swells in the stomach of the eater, making him feel as though he had waded through a Christmas dinner. Serve with mashed spuds and your victory will be complete! Children, especially, are very fond of this meal, because it has no bones, fat or gristle in it.

PICKLED HERRING

Pickled Herring is a useful standby in the summer, either as an *hors d'oeuvre* or as an easy lunch. But, like everything else, they must be good herrings to start with and they must be cooked properly. I have been given some, at times, that were enough to put anyone off for ever—fibrous and bony, with a flavour of raw fish still in them. A dozen herrings is a handy number for pickling because they will fit into the top of a small roasting tin without leaving space that would have to be filled with unnecessary liquid.

Spread a sheet of newspaper on the table and scatter some flour on it. Peel a small onion and chop it finely. Dust the boned herrings in the flour, sprinkle a pinch of onion over the inside, and then roll them up—skin side out. Pack them into a suitable sized container, in a single layer and with the dorsal fins uppermost. Distribute a teaspoonful of peppercorns and a couple of bay leaves in the crevices, and add some salt. Pour in malt vinegar until it comes half-way up the rolled herrings, and then add enough water to cover them. Bake in a slow to medium oven—without a lid—until the liquid is reduced to half, and the tops of the herrings have formed a dry "macintosh" of skin and flour. Put them in the larder to cool. I have never tried to eat them hot, but I should think they would be terrible. However, they are exceedingly good cold. When you eat them, the "macintosh", complete with dorsal fin, should come off in a piece, leaving a boneless, skinless, roll of fish.

* ❋ * ❋ * ❋ * ❋ * ❋ * ❋ *

PART FOUR

* ❋ * ❋ * ❋ * ❋ * ❋ * ❋ *

Beef

Mutton

Pork & Veal

Offals

CHAPTER VIII

❀

BEEF

"A JOINT of under 15-lbs. weight isn't worth putting in the oven." So said an old Yorkshire farmer to me many years ago. And, furthermore, he was right! The fact that it is quite unpractical to go around roasting enormous lumps of beef these pre-packed, vitaminised days has nothing to do with the truth of his statement. However, more of this later.

With meat as with most other things, one seldom gets both the ha'penny and the bun. Either it comes from a young animal and is very tender but has little flavour, or it comes from an older beast, with more taste but not so tender. The French chefs seem to prefer beef from a beast about five or six years old. The meat is then hung for a considerable time in a cool airy larder—not a fridge. When the maturing process has gone far enough—the meat tender and the flavour right—they take it out and use it. The fact that the same thing is not done in this country is largely the housewives' fault. Before Hitler's war a good butcher would not dream of letting meat go out of his shop until it was ready to cook. Hung for ten days, probably. Had he done otherwise his meat would have been tough and tasteless and his customers would have left him. During, and after the war a new generation of girls grew up and married. There was no meat, except for the odd scraps that constituted a "meat ration". They had no choice and no say in what they were buying, and anyway, how were they to learn? Their mothers had always relied on the butcher for the technical side of things, and therefore didn't know. The butcher, ashamed of having to sell such rubbish to his customers, was certainly not going to enlighten them and make them even more dissatisfied than they already were. They were used to getting "fresh" meat—bright red and with no scent at all—killed either that morning or the evening before. So, inevitably, after rationing was over and the customer could buy what she wanted, and as much of it as she chose, she went on getting the same stuff, only in bigger lumps. The butcher who tried to do his best by his customers by hanging properly would be told he could keep his dark-coloured, smelly old meat! So, faced with a demand for freshly-killed, tender meat, he has taken the only course open to him—to buy only very young animals. The fact that the meat is both expensive and tasteless does not seem to worry the customer, and the butcher is happy because he does not have to carry a large stock of highly perishable material. And that, as far as I can see, is how the matter stands —and how it will remain.

JOINTS & CUTS

Each part of the animal has, strangely enough, to be cooked in a different manner. It is not, as some people suppose, that one piece is inferior to another—is a pick inferior to a shovel?— but simply that they are used for different purposes. I will deal with the various cuts one by one, but the only way to learn them properly is to ask your butcher—some time when he is not busy!—to show them to you.

Roasts

These are usually taken from the back. "Sirloin" is the section between the pelvis and the floating ribs, and is considered to be the best of all. Certainly the Sovereign who boozily staggered to his feet and knighted it "Sir Loin" must have thought so! Then comes ribs of beef. This is really the same thing except that it does not have the "fillet" or undercut in it, and is taken from where the fillet ends, up towards the shoulder. Sometimes part of the upper leg, known as topside, is roasted. This is a very lean cut, with only a thin layer of fat round the outside and none in the muscle. It is therefore inclined to be rather dry, and a waste of a very fine piece of meat unless well larded.

Frying and Grilling

All this meat is the same as that used for roasting, only cut into smaller pieces. The undercut is taken out of the sirloin and cut into slices of between an inch and an inch-and-a-half thick to form "Chateau Briand" steaks, from the middle, and tournedos from the ends. Sirloin steak and entrecote steak is cut from the other, or upper side with the edging of fat around it. The only other piece which is used for frying, as far as I know, is the area lying behind the hip-bone and on top of the pelvis. This has many names—Best Steak, Rump Steak, Shell-bone Steak, etc. It is easy to recognise, being about sixteen inches long and five inches deep, and having a layer of fat along the top. The steak is cut off in slices of half-an-inch to an inch, according to what is wanted. If you are lucky—in other words, if the beast was a good one and was hung for the right length of time—this steak can be just as tender as undercut and with very much more flavour. Many experts consider that this cut is the best which can be taken off any animal. It is "Corner Gammon" in ham, and "Chump Chop" in mutton.

Casseroles and Stews (Cuts for)

Topside is probably the highest quality and most versatile cut in this category. As I have already said, it is sometimes roasted, but usually it is bought for high-quality casseroles, beef olives and similar purposes where a fine-grained meat which does not need too much cooking is required. It comes from the upper side of the thigh-bone, looked at as the side is hanging up; it has few, if any divisions in the muscle and is not cheap, the price charged being often the same as that for best steak.

Silverside is on the lower side of the thigh-bone and is usually used for pickling—"Boiled Beef and Carrots"! Very good it is too.

Shoulder is, in my opinion, the roughest part of the carcase. It is coarse-grained, dry and tough. It would make a passable stew and eatable mince but, apart from that, I would not buy it if I were you. Brisket, for me, comes in the same category, but perhaps I have been unlucky.

Shin or Hough is taken from the last 12 to 18 inches above the heel, in the hind leg, and the wrist in the front. It is here that the muscles begin to come into the tendon sheaths and the meat is very close-grained. It is surrounded by a whitish-yellow tissue of great strength, and also has this same substance running up into the lower part of the muscle itself—presumably to strengthen the join between muscle and tendon. I think the reason this cut is one of the cheapest must be because people will not cook it for long enough. Its flavour is superior to any-thing else for steak and kidney pie and similar uses—but it must be properly prepared and cooked for about four hours.

Flank and Brisket is sometimes salted or "pickled" and made into pressed beef, but I think that very often this, and any other bits and pieces—neck, etc.—is all ground up and made into beef sausages.

Beef Offals, i.e. Oxtail, Liver, Kidney, Sweetbreads, Skirt, Tongue and Brains, are all excellent if dealt with properly. Their treatment will be explained in a separate chapter.

Tripe. Having fed literally tons of this substance to mink and dogs—and also tried to eat it myself on one occasion—I have no hesitation in saying that although it may be edible to human beings, it certainly is not eatable. The feel of it in the mouth is revolting and it is completely tasteless.

Bones. These are of great value for making stock and a correctly-prepared marrow bone is a delicacy. Nobody bothers with them these homogenised days, so you can buy them for practically nothing.

ROASTING

The old farmer was quite right when he said that small pieces of beef were not worth putting in the oven. If you want roast beef for two or three people, get some steak and fry or grill it. If you put a piece of beef weighing two or three pounds into the heat needed to roast beef properly, either the inside will be about the correct shade of pink and the fat on the out-side practically raw, or, if you leave it in for longer, the fat on the outside will be done and the inside will be that odd grey colour as in "Roast and two veg., Luv". But, on the other hand, if the joint weighs from six pounds upwards, the outside will have time to cook properly without burning the fat, and the middle will be suitably underdone.

Explanation without demonstration is always difficult, especially so when colour and texture have to be described. First of all, ask the butcher what beef he has that was killed over a week ago—more still in the winter—and have it out for inspection. The fat should be nearly white and look to have an almost crumbly texture; the lean a darkish red with, if possible, a marbling of fat running through it. This marbling is usually found in meat from either Aberdeen-Angus or Hereford breeds. The advantage of it is that the lean is automatically basted all the way through as the meat cooks, and is therefore more likely to be tender. Sirloin is the equivalent of loin chops in lamb or pork, so see that the undercut or fillet has not been removed—both sides of the T-bone should be filled in with meat.

Rib is the same as an ordinary cutlet—one little round bit of meat stuck on the end of a long curved bone. If your rib is cut from too far towards the sharp end of the animal, you will see a streak of white cartilage about an eighth of an inch wide running through the meat midway between the outside and the bone. This is a rack or shoulder chop, which is usually inferior stuff.

The question of whether to have your sirloin or rib "on the bone" or rolled depends to a certain extent on the size of it, but to a larger degree on whether you trust your butcher or not. Never drink mild beer in a pub you don't know, and never buy rolled meat from a butcher you don't know! The temptation to pour the slops into the former, and to push a load of rubbish into the middle of the latter is sometimes irresistible. Very regrettable.

Anything less than three ribs is better rolled because a thicker, denser lump of meat will take longer to cook in the middle; but the larger joints not only look better left on the bone but taste better as well. Before you take either sirloin or rib out of the shop, ask the butcher if he will saw through the upper arm of the T for you, just clear of where it joins the centre. This is an enormous help when carving, as this flat plate of bone can easily be removed when the meat is cooked, and the entrecote—the side with the fat on—sliced up in comfort. Otherwise a lot of knife-blunting niggling to cut the slices out of the right angle is inevitable.

The actual roasting of the joint of beef is simplicity itself. All you need is a very hot oven, a roasting tin with a rack in it, a basting spoon, an oven cloth and—a watch! Meat, like—so I am told—everything else, should be cooked in a dying heat. The old bread ovens were a good example of this. They were built of brick, circular and domed inside, and were "fired" with dry gorse or brushwood until the bricks glowed with the heat. The ashes were then raked out and the bread put in. No further heat was needed, and I should think the results had to be tasted to be believed. Pity they don't still do it, instead of the steam-blasted sog that Mrs. Nineteen-Sixties takes home to her long-suffering, ulcerated husband.

As usual, the object of the exercise is to cook the outside as fast as possible without burning either the meat or the fat and the juices in the bottom of the tin—you will want those to make the gravy and if they are burnt, it will be black and bitter. The larger the joint, the easier it is to do this. As a general guide, allow a quarter of an hour per pound of beef. You will soon find out the balance between the heat of your oven and the amount you like the meat cooked, and can then of course, vary accordingly.

Place the joint on the rack in the roasting tin and put it in a very hot oven. The heat should not die away as much when cooking beef as with other meats, because the middle is intended to be undercooked, and the slow heat necessary to cook to the centre is not needed. Baste every half-hour, shutting the oven door immediately after taking the roasting dish out each time to avoid loss of heat as far as possible.

When roasting beef especially to be eaten cold, it should be cooked less than usual—only about ten minutes to the pound. Part of the reason for this is that the meat goes on cooking for some time as it cools.

The usual accompaniments are Yorkshire pudding, roast potatoes, any vegetable you please, horseradish sauce and gravy. The gravy is made by pouring most of the fat out of the roasting tin, scattering in some flour to make a *roux*, adding about half a pint of water and continuing boiling until, with frequent scraping and stirring, the mixture combines and thickens. Season.

CARVING

The first essential is a razor-sharp knife, and the second—especially if you are carving a roll—is a fork with an efficient guard on it. Stand the roll up on end and stick the fork into it at a downward angle of about 45 degrees and a third the way down from the top. Guard up. Carve in thin slices towards the fork, taking care not to let the knife touch it or the edge will not last long. To carve a sirloin or ribs, stand the joint on the dish with the fat uppermost. Carefully cut away the plate of bone that you asked the butcher to saw free for you. Stick the fork in the top and carve thin slices downwards to the bone, parallel to the ribs. The undercut is usually carved at right angles to the ribs and in half-inch slices. When carving *anything*, try as far as possible to save the edge of your knife from contact with the carving fork, bones and plate, thereby saving work and temper.

FRYING & GRILLING

The most expensive, and usually the tenderest, piece of beef is the undercut or fillet. These muscles lie along the loin, inside the rib-cage; they are roughly 18 inches long and taper from points at each end to about four inches thick in the middle. They weigh probably $2\frac{1}{2}$ to $3\frac{1}{2}$ lbs. each, so you will see that, compared with the half-ton of animal they come from, they cannot be said to be "in good supply". Hence the price, which, by the way, appears to be almost twice as much in the South of England as it is in the North. In fact, the only way you can be certain of getting this cut whenever you want it is to stumble across your butcher parked up a dark lane one night with the grocer's girl from next door!

Best steak is easier to come by, has a far better flavour, and can be just as tender—but usually isn't. Watch for the same points as when choosing sirloin, and try and have your slices cut from the centre of the lump; order it in advance.

A "Porterhouse" steak is a complete slice from the loin—bone and all—which accounts for its American name "T-bone". "Point" steak comes from the point or end of the "Best steak" lump.

Sirloin, contrefillet or entrecote steaks are all, as far as I can make out, the same thing—a thick slice from the upper side of the loin. It can be excellent if all the conditions are right, but it seems to be a cut which needs very expert handling before it is cooked, and therefore I would leave it to the Escoffiers of this world, and be content to eat the results.

A word of warning before we leave the subject of steak: there is not much real steak on a beast, and an increasing demand for what there is. It follows, therefore, that those who do not know what they are buying will get fobbed off with any piece of meat that can be trimmed up to look more or less like the genuine article. One of our local worthies had the reputation of being able to cut steaks off a cow up as far as the horns!

Cooking steak is very quick and very easy. Trim off all the fat—if you leave it on, it will be raw and uneatable—and any other untidy bits. Rub both sides with a cut garlic clove, and then grind a generous sprinkling of black pepper over them. Put only a dessertspoon of olive oil in the frying pan and heat it till a faint blue vapour comes off it. The reason for the olive oil, in preference to butter or an oil/butter mixture, is that olive oil boils at a higher temperature than most other edible fats, and therefore you can cook your steak faster without it taking on a taint of burning oil. A butter/oil mixture is often recommended; this is excellent for cooking a thick steak, such as an inch-and-a-half tournedo because, on the same principle as roasting a joint of beef, you have time to cook the outside properly without overdoing the middle. Butter burns at a comparatively low temperature and so I would not use it for steaks of between half-an-inch and an inch thick. Olive oil does the job more efficiently. Peanut (or ground-nut) oil is also very good, if it is of the highest quality. Excellent stuff for a deep frying pan, because it imparts no taste of its own whatsoever to anything fried in it. The ace fish-and-chip shops use it in spite of the cost—and make their fortunes.

In passing, it may be of interest to comment that the pundits recommend liquid vegetable oils, as opposed to solid animal fats, for cooking. They say one is less liable to drop down dead with a "Coronary"—which, in turn, reminds one of the rather cruel Top Executives' anthem:

> Ring a ring o' roses
> Coronary thrombosis
> Seizure
> Seizure
> All fall down!

In common with dogs, more men die of over-feeding than under-feeding.

Returning to the smoking frying-pan—put in the pieces of steak and press them down with the spatula. As soon as they are browned on one side, turn them over (having run the oil across the pan again first) and do the other side. Keep the stove at maximum reasonable heat whilst the meat is in the pan.

When grilling, paint the meat with melted butter and oil and cook it as fast as possible without burning it.

CASEROLES & STEWS

The basic principle of all these is the same, and any variation in the cut you buy or the thickness you have, depends on the particular dish you want to prepare. The only difference, as far as I know, between a stew and a casserole is the method of cooking it. A stew is put in a pot and cooked gently on the hob, or over a low flame; to make a casserole, the same contents are put in a fire-proof, covered, dish of some sort and cooked in the oven. The latter method is the better bet as a rule because there is less likelihood of burning or sticking, away from a direct flame.

I will give the ingredients, preparation and instructions for making an ordinary beef stew, and then try to show how it can be elaborated almost indefinitely.

Go and buy some topside. Avoid the very bright red meat if possible—choose the darker coloured sort with, if you're lucky, a marbling of fat in it. About half-an-inch thick. Put it on your chopping board and trim it up with a sharp knife, taking off what little fat there is and putting it in the dog's bowl. Cut into pieces about an inch square. If you allow half-a-pound per head you won't go far wrong and, anyway, you may as well make too much while you are about it, because it is even nicer the next day and will save you having to bother about grub tomorrow.

Peel one medium-sized onion per half-pound of beef, and a couple of smallish carrots. Slice the onion in half-inch rings, and the carrot in quarter-inch. Spread a newspaper on the kitchen table and tip half a cup of flour in the middle of it. Put your frying pan on the stove and pour some olive oil into it. Whilst the oil is heating, flour the onion rings and then fry them to a light golden colour. Put them in a layer in the pot or dish, followed by the carrots—usually unfried—in another layer. Flour and fry the pieces of beef till they are brown, and put them in too. Add salt, black pepper, a touch of cayenne pepper and, if you like, a couple of bay leaves or a teaspoon of thyme. Cover with boiling water and simmer—either on the stove or in the oven—for between 1½ and 2½ hours. When you can cut one of the bits of meat in half with a spoon, against the side of the pan, you can start taking the plates out of the oven and mashing the spuds. The stew should be of a rich brown colour with fairly thick gravy.

The best of all stewing beef is, in my opinion, shin or, as it is called in Scotland, hough. This, as I have explained earlier in this chapter, is taken from the lower part of the leg, either front or hind. The snags to it are, firstly, it takes quite a time to prepare and, secondly, it takes a long time to cook, but the texture and flavour—especially when used for steak and kidney pie—are superior to any other cut. Last, but by no means least, its price is little over half that of topside. To illustrate its treatment I will give you a receipt for:

Steak & Kidney Pie

Go and buy two to three pounds of shin beef from the part lowest down the leg. Don't let the butcher cut it up for you— take it home in a lump. Also get an ox kidney; this will weigh about a pound and so your ratio of beef to kidney will be about right. Use a very sharp knife with a rounded end for both the shin and the kidney. You will find, when you set to work on the shin, that it has a tough, semi-transparent skin covering the outside of it. By dint of a certain amount of patience, much tugging and some cutting underneath when it sticks, you get this off. Divide the meat up into the separate muscles of which it is composed—more tugging and cutting; trim off all the fat, the white tendon ends if they have been left too long, and any other bits you don't like the look of. You should now have four or five pieces of meat which look like small undercuts cut in half. Slice these up into half-inch discs, and cut the larger ones across again so that you end up with pieces of fairly even size.

Preparing the kidney is a fiddling job, but easy enough. It is almost certain to have had the membranous skin removed but, if it hasn't, remove it. I think the easiest way is to cut the kidney in half, lengthways, and then niggle away till you have cut out all the white centre away from the kidney, and left as little kidney as possible on the white centre. Cut it up into lumps slightly smaller than the shin. The dogs sit like supplicating sphinxes waiting for chunks of middle. Why it doesn't make them sick I don't know.

Flour and fry the whole issue, as for stew, and put it in a casserole. Water is perfectly all right as a cooking liquor, but I prefer beer. Draught beer, either bitter or mild will do, although I think I would rather use bitter—more used to it perhaps!

There is often no need to buy it even—your local Boozer would probably give you a pint of overspill or slops. As long as this is not sour, it does as well as anything else. Seasoning is, as usual, a matter of taste. My own view is that the flavour of this dish is of such excellence that it is quite unnecessary to tart it up with garlic and herbs. I put in salt, black pepper and cayenne pepper, and leave it at that.

Put it in the oven and bring to the boil; then reduce heat till it is just bubbling and keep it there for three hours. Take it out and try to cut a piece of shin against the side of the casserole with a spoon. You probably won't be able to, but it will give you some idea of how it's getting on. Stir up gently and replace in the oven. It will be done in four to five hours. As soon as you can cut the meat, tip it out into the pie-dish you intend to use and put it in the larder to cool.

The pastry is made in the same way as for rabbit pie, in other words, by your Tame Pastry-Maker. A phone call will, with a bit of luck, have her panting on the doorstep within ten minutes—a bag of flour clutched in one fist and a rolling-pin in the other—rarin' to go!

Swing straight into the Gin and Soft-soap routine. But remember—DON'T kiss her till she has carried out her duties; otherwise you will find the situation gets completely out of hand and you end up, hours later, with no gin and no lid on your pie!

Beef Olives

This dish is another variation on the basic theme, but different enough and pleasant enough to be included among the demonstration pieces.

You use topside again. Have it sliced a quarter of an inch thick—if you tell the butcher what you want it for, he will take more trouble to cut it evenly.

In most dishes there is a fiddling bit, and in this case it is making the stuffing. The amount of running around that is needed to find all the ingredients makes the list look rather like the instructions for a treasure hunt:

2-oz. suet

2-oz. ham

4-oz. fresh breadcrumbs

1 dessertspoon parsley (chopped)

A pinch of mixed herbs

Grated rind of half a lemon

Salt and pepper

Raw beaten egg to bind

Chop or mince the suet and the ham and mix in a bowl with the breadcrumbs and other gubbins. Beat up an egg, tip it in, and mix. If not a solid, claggy consistency, mix another egg in. You will find that these quantities go nowhere, so if you have more than two people to feed, double them.

Trim the meat and cut it into rectangles about three inches wide by four long. Spread the stuffing on the meat so that both are about the same thickness. Roll up each piece carefully and secure by tying with thin string, a third the way in from each end. Alternatively, a lazier and not so efficient method is to skewer with cocktail sticks at the same points.

Flour and fry the olives in exactly the same way as for everything else in this section. Put them in a casserole, cover with water, stock, beer, wine, cider—just as you like—and simmer gently in the oven for about a couple of hours.

Another method is to make one enormous olive instead of many small ones, and carve it into bits before serving. I can't see much advantage in it myself.

This dish is especially useful for cold winter evenings when your guests are likely to be delayed by snow and ice on the roads, or lured by warm lights and a roaring fire into a wayside inn en route. Put it in a warm oven and it will not spoil for two or three hours.

Norwegian Meat Balls

This is a useful form of casserole which gives infinite scope for variation in flavouring. The meat balls can be made so that very young children will enjoy them, garlicked till a Chasseur will wolf them amid "Magnifiques", or peppered so that they choke an Indian Army colonel.

Buy equal amounts of lean beef—anything will do except

perhaps shin—and belly pork. If you allow half-a-pound per head there will be any amount. Ask the butcher to trim the bits of gristle out of the pork, and then put it all through his mincer—twice—alternating the beef and pork to get a thorough mix the first time.

Put the mince in a big mixing-bowl and then accumulate the following gubbins:

Dried breadcrumbs (bread dried in the oven and then crushed into crumbs with a rolling-pin or a mincer)

Chopped parsley; finely chopped onion; finely chopped garlic;

One raw egg for each pound of meat.

Cayenne pepper; black pepper; salt; mixed herbs.

(Tomato purée and chopped hard-boiled egg is a useful alternative when mild flavouring is needed).

Scatter in all the seasonings and break the eggs on top. Then, with a big fork, start stirring and mixing, meanwhile sprinkling in the breadcrumbs. If you want to use a higher proportion of crumbs and the mixture is already at the stiff claggy stage, add a little milk. Mix away till everything is properly combined. The technique reminds one inevitably of using a concrete mixer—a drop of water if too stiff, and another shovel of cement if too sloppy!

When the right degree of rigidity has been achieved, scoop small lumps up with a spoon. Fashion them into balls about the size of a squash-ball, and roll them in flour. It always surprises me how many the bowlful makes.

From here onwards the process is exactly the same as the other casseroles. Being stuck together with egg, the balls will not disintegrate even if cooked for hours, but remember, the longer a thing is cooked the fainter will become the seasonings you have put in; until in the end all you can taste will be a little hotness from the cayenne pepper.

Fat bacon may be used instead of pork, and makes the meat a red colour due to the action of the saltpetre used in bacon curing. Don't put as much salt in—there is probably enough in the bacon.

From these four examples hundreds of variations can be

concocted. Dried fruit and peas and beans can be added, besides fresh ones. *Vegetables* of all kinds can be put in to a stew at such a time as to ensure that they will be properly cooked when the meat is ready. If they are added at the beginning they will be cooked to destruction. *Dumplings* are a very useful standby in the stew department, being really lumps of pud of the same kind as the basin is lined with in a steak and kidney pudding. They are made like this:

Dumplings

To each half-pound of self-raising flour, mix in three ounces of grated suet (home-made or bought). Add pepper and salt and mix to a stiff paste with water. Herbs can also be added if you like. Roll into balls the size of a squash-ball and drop into the boiling stew half-an-hour before it is served. Alternatively, boil for half-an-hour in stock or salt water.

From dumplings we move on, inevitably, to the last section in this chapter.

Boiled Beef

Boiled beef and dumplings, or boiled beef and carrots are almost as traditional as the Roast Beef of Old England itself.

For this purpose the beef is always pickled; this process is usually left to the butcher, who will have a pickling tub always on the go. But if you wish to do it yourself, put a mixture of salt and saltpetre (about 25 parts salt to one of saltpetre) in an earthenware crock and keep topping up with water and mixture until you have enough saturated solution of pickle to cover your lump of beef. Leave it there for at least five days, and not more than seven.

The cuts used for this purpose are silverside, which comes from the lower side of the thigh-bone as the carcase is looked at hanging up. Brisket, from the sternum or breast-bone, and rolled flank—which I would avoid if I were you, unless the butcher is a particular chum of yours.

Soak the meat in cold water, preferably running, for some

hours to get the surplus salt out of it, and then boil for half-an-hour to the pound. Prepare your carrots, onions and dumplings, putting them in at their proper cooking time from zero hour, when the beef is done. Roughly, onions and carrots one-and-a-half hours, and dumplings half-an-hour.

Serve with creamed potato and put some of the cooking liquor in a gravy boat on the table.

Before we leave the subject, I would like to be sure that you have got what is meant by "boiling" quite straight in your mind. The only time that I can think of when food is boiled hard and continuously is in the reduction of a cooking liquor before making a sauce or gravy. Otherwise all meats and fish should be put into fast boiling water, salted if the thing to be cooked is not already salt. As soon as the water comes to the boil again, reduce heat until the water is just moving in the pan and swirling on the top. Keep it there for the rest of the cooking time. This is what is known as "poaching". Water, unless under pressure, cannot get any hotter than 100° C. It turns into steam after that, so the object of the exercise is to adjust the heat so that it will stay at 100° C. without boiling away. There are two advantages in this: one is that the pot does not need topping up so often, and the other that the lower the flame the less likely are the contents of your pan to stick to the bottom and burn. It is generally accepted that meat which is boiled fast turns out to be tough, and that meat which is simmered will be tender. I agree that this is usually correct, but I cannot see any good reason why it should be so. The temperature—100° C.—is, to all intents and purposes, the same, and the only difference that I can see is the increased mechanical agitation caused by rapidly rising bubbles of steam in the former case, as opposed to the slower movement in the latter.

* ❀ *

CHAPTER IX

MUTTON

It seems that, in common with wines and some fruit, mutton is at its best when it comes from areas where life is by no means easy, and the sheep have had a struggle to stay alive at all in the winter. Scotch Blackface, Welsh Mountain, Rough Fell and Swaledale are all excellent, but to my mind the one that beats the lot is the Herdwick from the Cumbrian and North Lancashire fells. The pure-bred lamb is black as soot when born, goes brown at about a year old, and finally grey with a white muzzle when full grown. Small and incredibly agile, they are a nightmare to gardeners in the Spring when there is very little grass about. In fact one distinguished Air Force officer, infuriated beyond bearing at the sight of the total destruction of his garden, emptied his revolver into one of the culprits. Unfortunately, a new and unsympathetic village bobby happened to be cycling past, behind the hedge, just at that moment. Meat rationing was in force, and there was a lot of bother about it.

The origin of the Herdwick is the subject of conjecture and, sometimes, heated argument. One widely held theory is that they were carried as live food supply on the Spanish Armada. When some of the galleons were wrecked on the Cumberland coast, the sheep are thought to have swum ashore and taken to the fells where, being mountain sheep anyway, they settled in and lived happily ever after. It is said that identical sheep can be seen in Spain to this day. Opponents of the Armada idea say "Absolute poppycock! No galleons ever were wrecked on the Cumberland coast—and even if they had been, the time lag is such that food would have run desperately low by the time the ships got away round here, and the sheep would all have been eaten anyway". Personally, I rather like the story, accurate or not. The fact remains, however, that Herdwick mutton, Spanish or native, killed in the autumn and well hung, is unbeatable for both flavour and texture.

Whilst it is exceedingly unlikely, in this country, that you will ever have to knock off, and dress out, a live sheep to get a couple of chops for your supper, I had better—following the "First Principles" idea of this book—give instructions for the operation.

Put a bullet, or humane killer bolt, at right angles through the sheep's skull, in the centre of the forehead and an inch above the level of the eyes. Lay the carcase on its back on a low trestle or bench, with the head hanging over the end. It may still be kicking, but if you have made a proper job with the rifle, it will be as dead as the proverbial mutton. Now, with a razor-sharp knife, sever the jugular. A deep swift cut under the jawbone, on the left hand side will do this. The heart will still beat for long enough to clear the carcase of blood. This must be done, or the meat will not keep.

Take your skinning-knife, and open the skin the whole way down from the throat to the vent. Don't cut too deep and go through the abdominal wall. Cut the skin also along the insides of the thighs as far as the hocks. Take off all the feet, the front ones at the wrists or "knees", and the hind ones just below the hocks—leaving the Achilles tendons intact.

Now skin out the hindquarters, using your thumbs and knife handle to work the pelt away from the meat, and also expose the rib cage. With a bone saw, open up the chest by cutting down the middle of the sternum or brisket. Look inside and find the weasand, which is the food pipe running from the stomach to the oesophagus, where it joins in with the windpipe. It is red in colour and about as thick as your finger. Cut it at the throat end, take it out of the chest, and tie a knot in the end of it. The reason for doing this is so that the stomach contents cannot regurgitate when the carcase is hung upside down. Put a stretcher—a piece of wood with notches cut in it to keep the hocks apart—through the Achilles tendons, and hang the carcase up so that the head is about eighteen inches off the ground. A couple of meat-hooks will do if you haven't got a stretcher. Complete the skinning by pulling the pelt down, skinning out the front legs and cutting away at the back of the head. Now slit the abdomen up. Cut away the "pluck", which consists of the windpipe, lungs, heart and liver—all joined together. Hang this up separately. Remove all the rest of the inside, with the exception of the kidneys, and bury it. Cut off the head and trim out the anal tunnel.

Wipe the carcase down with a damp cloth and hang it in a cool, bluebottle-free larder. A good slaughterman does this whole job in an incredibly short time—well under five minutes —whilst chattering away to his buddy next door about the football match last Saturday.

If you can, it is always better to hang meat in a complete carcase, rather than separate joints. Apart from the tendency of small bits to dry faster, the maturing process seems to be more even in a larger lump.

After a week or more, the time will come when you have to cut the carcase up and eat it, deep-freeze it, sell it, give it away, or what have you. Mutton, unlike beef or pork, is left round, instead of being cleft down the spine and turned into sides. Get your largest butcher's knife and a bone-saw, lay the carcase on a bench or table, and cut round with the knife just above the hip-bones. Saw through the spine transversely. Take the hind legs, which you have thus detached, turn them with the shanks towards you, and saw up the middle of the spine, longitudinally. This is not as easy as it sounds, but is made simpler if you have someone else there to help hold it steady. Cut in again just below the ribs, and saw off the saddle. This can be left as it is if you are going to have a party with Saddle of Lamb as the high spot. I agree that this is all very nice, and makes one think of bustles and fans, of jingling spurs and the clatter of hooves on cobbles. But a saddle is not an easy joint to carve, and therefore inclined to be wasteful. Also it is not so hot cold! So I would advise you to reach for the saw again. Cut on up the spine till you have produced two pieces of Loin from the saddle.

Unless you want the carving of the loin to be an undignified brawl—probably with the dog as the main beneficiary when the joint flies off the dish—it must be "cracked", as the butchers call it. They, with years of practice behind them, sit the joint up on its sawn flat and, with strokes of a small cleaver, break each half-vertebrae clear of the next. I don't recommend you to try it. I once halved the carcase of a young goat with a felling-axe. It ended up in two bits all right, but I had no strong desire to enter it in a craftsmanship exhibition! A sound, if less showy, method of cracking is to *place* the tip of the cleaver—or the chopper from the wood-shed will do as well—in the joint between two vertebrae, and bash the back of it with a large hammer or lump of rock. Trim off the flap of belly and hang the two bits of loin up beside the legs. Of course, if you want to make a particularly ritzy job of it, you can always saw the vertebrae free of each other—but this is a tedious business.

You are left now with the rib-cage and front legs. Chop off the neck, and then saw the cage in two, down the centre of the spine. It is already opened up down the front. The shoulders can be taken off simply by running the knife between them and the ribs, but it is more usual to saw out the section of ribs to which the foreleg is attached, and roast the lot as Shoulder of Mutton. All that remains after this are chops and breast of mutton. Starting from the loin end of the ribs, you take off the cutlets. These are the ones which used to be trimmed down until only a round piece of meat was left at the end of a long bone with a paper frill round it. Then you come to the rack, or chine chops. These are larger and have a streak of gristle in them. To separate chops, cut down between the ribs with the knife, severing everything except the bone. Cut this either with saw or cleaver.

Having reduced our sheep to the familiar joints of mutton you see in the butcher's shop, I will go on to explain the basic methods of cooking the various pieces. As usual, you can embroider indefinitely—especially with the help of a cookery book by one of the Masters. Escoffier, for instance, who is accepted even by professional chefs as the ultimate authority.

LEG OF MUTTON

Leg of Mutton shares with the loin the pride of place as the best cuts on the carcase, but it must be hung for a longer time than meat from other animals, except perhaps deer. If I can, I hang a leg till it reminds my nose of its presence when I go into the larder. Then I wash it in cold water to which salt and vinegar has been added. This completely removes the pong. If it is cooked too fresh it lacks flavour and is inclined to be a bit tough.

Spring lamb, which comes into the shops in the early summer is, of course, very tender—and pretty expensive—but it has a soft texture which I don't care about, and very little flavour. Yet another case of personal preference.

Roast Leg of Mutton

If the shank bone has not already been cut, saw it through just below the point where the meat ends, and double it back. You have the choice of roasting the leg plain, *au naturel,* or whatever you like to call it; or else you can spike it with garlic. To do this, peel two or three cloves (of garlic) and then, with a very sharp knife, split them lengthways into four or five slivers. Prod holes with a knife point, in the mutton and insert the pieces at intervals all over the surface of the joint. When half cooked, sprinkle with rosemary leaves. It is worth while finding out first of all whether any of your guests loathe garlic—some people do.

There is very little to say about the actual roasting. Start off with a hot oven to seal the meat, and then reduce heat till the joint is just sizzling. Baste at least every hour to prevent drying and to ensure that the outside is crisp. Overcook a bit. The flavour is improved, and the meat is more tender. The French often serve mutton half-raw—as pink as beef—but I don't like it. A leg usually takes about two-and-a-half hours, but you can tell when it is done by the way the meat recedes from the bone. Remove from the roasting tin and place on dish in the simmering oven. Pour most of the fat off the liquid in the tin, scatter in a dessertspoon of flour, stir and press out the lumps. Allow to cook for a few minutes, and then add some of the boiling water from a vegetable pan. Continue boiling and adding water till you have a gravy of the consistency you like.

Onion sauce, or, as some people call it, creamed onions, is a great addition to this dish. Roughly chop two or three large onions and boil them till tender. Pour off the liquid. Make a fairly stiff white sauce (Instructions in Chapter 7) well salted and peppered, and stir the onion into it. Put a jar of red-currant jelly on the table too.

Boiled Leg of Mutton

Boiled Leg of Mutton doesn't seem to be as popular as it used to be. For some curious reason it appears to be looked down on as rather a plebian dish. However, if you have acquired a large leg of pretty rough old stuff, I would strongly advise you to boil it with carrots and onions till it is tender—start off with half-an-hour to the pound and then carry on till prodding tells you it is edible. Serve with caper sauce—which is simply a white sauce with capers stirred into it. Save the stock from the boiling to make Scotch Broth.

LOIN

Loin is a good excuse for making a pig of oneself. Although it is probably the best piece of the carcase when eaten hot, it is most disappointing cold. Therefore, buy rather more than you really need, and whack in!

As far as I know, it is always roasted. It would be impossible to find a better way of cooking it anyhow. If there is too much fat on it, whittle some away till there is only about half-an-inch depth left. The object to be aimed at is to have the fat cooked crisp, so that it is eatable, and a minimum of nauseating white lumps. In order to do this, a certain amount of over-cooking is unavoidable; but, as I have said before, I think the flavour is improved. The trimmings are the same as for roast leg.

SHOULDER

Shoulder is usually rather fat—intermuscular—and so it should be roasted very slowly for a long time, to allow this fat time to melt and run out. Otherwise the form is the same as previously. Although it is more difficult to carve, I would advise you to buy shoulder on the bone, rather than rolled. It cooks better and you know what you are getting.

CHOPS

Chops come in four different kinds: Chump, loin, cutlets and rack. I will deal with them one at a time.

A chump chop is taken from the top end of the leg between the tail and the hip-bone. It is the meat covering the half-pelvis, and is the same as Best Steak from an ox, or Corner Gammon off a pig. The piece—it is only about six inches long—should be boned, and any lumps of fat cut away. Then it is cut into slices of the thickness required. The resulting chop is very lean, of excellent quality, and can be grilled, fried, braised or casseroled.

Loin chops are single vertebrae from the loin of lamb that we have already roasted earlier in this chapter. They sometimes have a piece of the kidney in them. Although they are very nice fried or casseroled, I always feel it is rather a waste when they are so much better roasted in a piece.

Cutlets, left untrimmed, are the traditional "chop", and probably the best for frying, mixed grills, etc. but, of course, are quite suitable for a casserole too.

Rack chops are, to my mind, the poor relation in the chop family, like a song title of many years ago, "Rough, Tough and Unattractive". They are best stewed or put in a Tatie Pot. Finally, all you have left is neck and breast of mutton. Neck is divided into best-end and scrag-end. Both these are used for Irish Stews and Tatie Pots. Breast is the meat on the rib-cage after the bones have been taken out. It is used for stews and sometimes spread with stuffing and rolled, to make a pleasant, if somewhat greasy casserole.

Joe, my old Spaniel, lying snoring under my desk, and his irrepressible grandson trying to climb on my knee in order to stuff his nose in the typewriter, reminds me—sheep heads! If you have a puppy to bring up, there is nothing better that you can feed it on, from the time it is weaned till it is about nine months old, than sheep heads several times a week. Another advantage is that if you don't get them for nothing, they ought only to cost sixpence each. The only snag is the time and fiddling about involved, but the results produced will prove to you that it hasn't been wasted. Try to get the skulls already cleft, but if you fail to do this, place the head on a tree-stump or block and cleave it, in true XII century style, with a single blow of your trusty chopper. Pretending to yourself that it is, in fact, the head of one of the Jacks-in-office who needlessly complicate life these days, will turn the crack of shattering bone and spatter of brains from nausea to satisfaction! Put the remains in an old iron pot and simmer until the meat is falling off the bones. Take it out, put it on a big dish and pick the skull clean with a knife and fork. It is surprising the amount that comes off. Chop it up, tongue and all, and mix it with the same volume of wheaten biscuit meal, then pour on enough of the stock to make the mixture fairly sloppy. Feed it warm if possible; you will find it disappears like a flash. Put the bones on a tin tray and bake them in the oven till they are brittle. This may take several days. Then grind them up in a mortar to the consistency of coarse oatmeal. Mix this bonemeal into the next day's food and tip in a dessertspoon of veterinary cod-liver oil. I have found that this system will produce all the bone, teeth and coat that one could wish for. If you feed fish (cod fillets that have "gone off" and are therefore cheap) stewed in milk, on the other days, you will make assurance doubly sure. During meat rationing I made a sheep's head pie for myself. After one slice, Joe got the rest! I will not include it among the receipts.

If I give you four widely-differing methods of cooking mutton, you can alter and adapt them to your own requirements and, with the help of a little imagination, do as well as, or better than the text-books.

In the Lake District of Cumberland, Westmorland and Lancashire North o' the Sands, the most famous of all dishes is the Tatie Pot. Whether it is a Shepherd's Meet, Hunt Meeting, Local Dales Show, or just a boozy night out, the pub nearest to the scene of action will produce enormous stew-jars and roasting tins full of Tatie Pot—which is just as well, because the quantity of the stuff that the lads, who have spent the day on the fell and the night in the bar, can put away, would make you goggle! Each landlord's wife is convinced that no one can make it properly bar herself, but the basic receipt is fairly simple:

TATIE POT

Take one medium-sized sheep (preferably somebody else's) and reduce it to handy-sized pieces.

Peel the sack of spuds that a local farmer gave you after you had been wondering, out loud, who had torn half Edith Entwhistle's frock off at the last hop.

Skin and chop those two straps of onions that you pinched off his pole when that Breton onion-seller was in the bar last week.

Cut up the black pudding that your dog nicked out of the back whilst the butcher was tinkering with the engine of the ramshackle old banger he euphemistically calls a Mobile Shop.

You are now, in the vernacular, fit up.

Into the largest containers that will fit into your oven, put alternating layers of sliced potato, mutton and black pud. and onion. Scatter plenty of salt and pepper in as you go along. After all, you aren't in business for fun and you want the lads to "git suppin'" again after t'tatie pot! Fill up with boiling water and put in the oven. Allow to simmer away for hours. In fact, some tatie-pot whallopers insist that it be cooked the day before and re-simmered on the day of the binge.

One of our local landlords came rather badly unstuck a couple of years ago. A member of the Hunt Committee came along and asked that a tatie-pot supper be laid on for a certain evening, when the Annual Meeting was going to be held. Now the dalesmen has many virtues, but Organisation (with a capital O) is not one of them. Unknown to this chum, another of his ninety-nine fellow committee men had gone to another pub about ten miles away, and done the same thing. The first berk forgot all about his order, and didn't tell anyone else.

And so, on the magic night, with literally half a hundredweight of tatie-pot bubbling in the oven, nobody turned up. For the next week the family ate it, the neighbours ate it, the old-age pensioners ate it, the dog ate it—and the hens, and the ducks. I cannot say whether the cause of all the trouble has dared to show his nose inside the door again yet, but if he has it must be only very recently!

These huge Hunt and Agricultural Show committees always strike me as an excellent advertisement for Independents in Government. A considerable proportion of the members detest a considerable proportion of other members. Their families have probably not been on speaking terms since the Napoleonic Wars (the reason long since forgotten). Therefore, in an atmosphere of minimum co-operation, nothing gets done. It seems that, whichever of our Great Parties is in power, legislation is mostly penal, and against the interests of the Subject; and most of the world-shaking decisions turn out to have been the wrong ones. So it would seem to follow that if the House were full of Independents, they might, with a bit of luck, be too busy fighting among themselves to find time to push our noses any further in the mire, or get us into any more trouble abroad with their "diplomacy".

"A far step, my friend" you may say "from tatie-pots to Whitehall"—you may indeed be right! The cobbler will return forthwith to his last.

The Lancashire Hot-pot is another variation on the theme. It is, I think, usually made with beef and has additional layers of carrot and sometimes turnip put in. In fact, unless you are going to feed it to a reactionary bunch of bucolic connoisseurs, you can put anything you like in it.

FRENCH FRIED CUTLETS

French Fried Cutlets are rather a special dish. One to be reserved for occasions when you are dining rich Great-aunt Agatha, or jockeying for position with a new girl-friend. The innocent look of it on the plate, with its pleasantly-coloured little piles of vegetables, has an old-word charm and serenity that belies your black heart, beating its Machiavellian tattoo under that Savile Row jacket! "The dear boy. Anyone with the imagination and sensitivity to produce such a tasteful meal would be absolutely incapable of any base thought or action." Little do they know!

Cutlets are rather small, and quite a lot of them is trimmed off, so be sure you buy enough. Cut away all the fat, leaving the round piece of lean at the top. Beat up an egg and dip the cutlet, which has already been very lightly dusted with flour, in it. Then roll it in breadcrumbs and fry for about five minutes on each side in olive oil. It should now have an attractive golden appearance. If it is still possible to get cutlet frills, the Good Old Days illusion would be heightened. Before you fried the cutlets you would have made some Espagnole sauce. This is one of the two basic sauces from which a very large proportion of all the others are made.

ESPAGNOLE SAUCE

Chop up two onions, one large carrot and two ounces of lean bacon. Fry them in two ounces of butter (or a butter/olive oil mixture) till they are a rich brown colour. Scatter in a heaped tablespoon of flour and continue frying till the flour has gone golden. Now add half-a-pound of tomatoes (canned, I find are best) a glass of white wine and one-and-a-half pints of stock. Bring to the boil, stirring continuously. Lastly put in what is known as a "bouquet garni"—which consists, in this case, of some parsley, a pinch of thyme and a bay leaf. Simmer, without the lid, for an hour, stirring now and again to prevent sticking. Finally strain into a clean pan, pressing the mixture round the strainer with a spoon to squeeze as much liquid as possible through. Simmer slowly for another half hour and you've finished. If the sauce is a bit sloppy, boil it away some more; and if too thick, add more stock to it.

As a matter of interest, the following sauces all have Espagnole as their base: Bordelaise, Chasseur, Bigarade, Perigueux, Portugaise, Red-currant Jelly, Reforme and Robert. There will be many others as well.

I would suggest that you get a bottle of white Beaujolais, put one glass in the sauce, and drink the rest at dinner. They will be feeding out of your hand after that!

MUTTON CASSEROLE

Mutton Casserole (or Stew) is an extremely good winter dish, is easy to make, and uses any cut of meat—provided it is not too fat. Chump chops are probably the best form, but neck, rack chops or breast will do almost as well.

The day before you intend to operate put a couple of handfuls of dried haricot beans (or, better still, dried red Mexican beans if you can get them) and one of dried peas, to soak in cold water. See that you have not run out of onions and carrots. Some outer stems of celery are a help too. Chop all the vegetables to a half-inch to inch size and fry them either in oil or in mutton dripping you have rendered out of the fat cut off the meat. Scatter a spoonful of flour over them as they cook. Stir them up and scatter in another spoonful. Continue frying and stirring till the mixture starts to brown. Transfer into a casserole and add the beans and peas. Flour and fry the mutton; when it is browned properly, bury it in the bed of vegetables. Add cayenne, marjoram and salt; fill up with boiling water—or better still, beer or cider—and put in the oven on a low heat and simmer for a couple of hours. Of course, if it is a stew, bring to the boil and then simmer on top of the stove. Like most dishes of this type, it will very likely have a better flavour if you cook it one day and then bring it slowly to the boil the next day when you want to use it. During the cooling and re-heating processes the flavour seems, in some odd way, to blend and mature.

If you put plenty of vegetables in to start with, you will only need to make some mashed spuds and your meal is ready.

Mutton is not an easy meat to do anything with when it is cold. Rissoles and shepherd's pie made with it have to be seasoned up till they make your ears flap or they taste "muttony". It is a traditional basis for curry, but, personally, I would much rather use either beef or pork. And so, apart from good cold leg of mutton and pickles, I would advise you to arrange things so that there is none left over.

The fourth receipt, which I mentioned earlier, is as different from the others as I can make it. Very cheap to make, and will feed an army.

STUFFED ROAST BREAST OF MUTTON

Buy the mutton in as large pieces as possible and, if it has not already been boned, take the bones out with a sharp, pointed knife. Work from the inside and cut in at an angle down the edge of each bone, from both sides, and lift it out. Make a stuffing consisting of the following:

1-oz. suet	Large pinch of marjoram
2-ozs. chopped bacon	Grated rind of half a lemon
5-ozs. fresh breadcrumbs	Raw beaten egg to bind
1 tablespoon chopped parsley	Salt and pepper.

Mix all this together to a stiff paste, using milk to moisten if a couple of eggs are not enough. This quantity would be enough for about a pound of meat, so increase when necessary. Spread the meat with stuffing to the same thickness as the meat itself, and roll it up. Tie with fine string at three-inch intervals to keep body and soul together and roast in a covered tin—slowly. It can be floured and fried and then casseroled, but is very greasy done in this manner. If, on the other hand, it is roasted (or to be precise, baked) the excess fat has time to run out during the cooking period.

A good antidote to richness, or greasiness, in a dish made with mutton is pickled cabbage. It is very easy to make. Sharpen up your largest chef's vegetable knife till it is like a razor. Cut a firm, sound red cabbage in quarters, lengthways, and then slice up the quarters as finely as you can, crossways. Cut out the rough bit of stalk. Spread the result—which looks like bloodstained sauerkraut—on a large dish and sprinkle salt and a little saltpetre (to preserve the colour) over it. After a few hours, turn it over and sprinkle more salt. About twenty-four hours later, pour off any liquid that has run out. Divide a packet of pickling-spice (chemist) into four and tie each lot up in a little piece of muslin. A bit of that old net curtain of Auntie's will do! Drop one into each jar before cramming it tight with cabbage. Fill up with ordinary cold malt vinegar— and Bob's your Uncle! Ready to use in a few days.

✿

CHAPTER X

PORK & VEAL

✿

PORK

THE pig, with its almost infinite versatility, could fill a cook-book of its own. So I do not propose to wade through Large Whites, Gloucester Old Spots, Tamworths and Landraces. Neither will I attempt a treatise on pig-killing or bacon-curing. I don't know enough about it for a start, and I expect H.M. Stationery Office have covered the subject, with their usual efficiency.

For most practical purposes you can regard pork in much the same way as mutton. The various cuts, and their uses, are similar; the main difference being that a pig is not skinned. After it had been stunned, by either electricity or gas, and "stuck"—by which time it is, of course, dead—the carcase is dipped in boiling water, and then scraped. This removes the hair and dirt, and it only remains to disembowel and cleave in half. When I was a lad, I remember watching an old man trying, with very little success, to shave his "cottager's pig" with a blunt cut-throat razor. Evidently the water he had used for scalding had not been hot enough.

When stewing, the skin is cut off, but if there is a joint to be roasted, the object of the exercise is to get the crackling to crackle. This is by no means as easy as it sounds because, when you repeat a treatment that worked last time, you will find that it often doesn't work this time! Acting on instructions from various crackling cracklers, I have rubbed the skin with salt, with olive oil, with salt *and* olive oil, with sugar and salt; I have sprinkled it with flour. Except for the flour technique, the others have all worked at times—but not at others. I am yet to be convinced that the successful efforts would not have been just as successful if they had been left untreated. In other words, I think that some pieces of pig-skin will crackle easily and others won't, and all this rubbing with secret liniments, so much mumbo-jumbo. You might as well rub them on your own backside for all the good they will do!

I discovered what I think to be the answer quite by accident. I had roasted a large leg of pork—it looked and smelt marvellous —but the skin was smooth and shiny, and about as edible as a sjambok. I had an idea, and went down to the workshop and lighted a painter's blow-lamp. Taking the joint outside, still in the roasting tin, I started to play the tip of the flame over it. First of all I burnt a piece black, so quick was the effect, but I found that by keeping the visible tip of the flame two inches away from the target, the rhinoceros-hide turned quickly to crackling of a light biscuit-like texture. From this, my dear Watson, we deduce that the form is to roast slowly, as for mutton; then to remove the joint from the oven and make the gravy with the unburnt juices from the meat. Meanwhile the oven is heating to maximum. Replace joint in furnace for just long enough to achieve the desired result. It works, too!

Pork is a meat which should not be hung for long. Three days in the summer, and a week in the winter is plenty. I suppose it is for this reason, coupled with the revolting stuff a pig will eat, that accounts for the banning of pork to Jews and Mohammedans. There weren't many fridges in Moses' day! Also remember that pork, in any form, MUST be very well cooked. I won't go into grisly details, but you can take it from me that it is so.

Pork chops are usually better floured and fried, and then casseroled. They often tend to be a bit dry if just fried. This does not apply, of course, to a roast loin of pork.

Stewed pork forms a basis for any number of dishes; the Chinese technique of adding very finely-sliced, and very lightly-cooked vegetables to the already cooked pork, is a particularly good one, but the primary recipe is:

Cut the meat in cubes, taking out the fat and putting it in the frying pan to render down. Flour the cubes (in cornflour, if you want a clearer gravy) and fry in the fat you will have in the frying pan. Slice, lightly flour, and lightly fry some onion and whatever other vegetables you wish to use, and then either simmer or casserole slowly, till tender.

PORK SAUSAGE

There are, as they say, bangers and bangers! If I were you I would systematically work my way round all the different makes of sausage, and all the local butchers who make their own sausage, until I found one that I liked. Some have so much fat in them that you end up with a pan-full of grease and a banger the thickness of your little finger. Others are mostly meal—have lumps of gristle in them—have a flavouring you don't like—are too rough cut—are too fine cut—have skins of indestructible plastic—split too easily, and so on *ad infinitum*. Having found what you want, whether it is in separate sausages, or looks as if it was sold by the foot, take a carving fork and prod double holes about half-an-inch apart all the way along both sides. Put only a scrap of fat in the frying-pan, because even the best sausage will make quite enough fat to cook itself, and sausage-fat is of no further use, except to pour over dried bread or biscuits for the dogs. This is all very well once in a while—and much appreciated—but don't do it too often, as fat is not particularly good for dogs.

Sausages come into the Slowly for a Long Time category. When they start sizzling, turn down the heat so that they continue in the same way—no spitting crescendo accompanied by clouds of blue smoke! After about ten minutes the side of the banger which is getting the treatment ought to be the colour of a well-polished brown shoe. Turn it over carefully, and when you hear a sudden increase in the noise from the frying-pan— probably in another ten minutes—it will be cooked.

My qualifications for pontificating on the subject of banger-bashing date from the age of thirteen. Our unspeakable House-master, having fed us during the week with all the luxury of a Dickensian orphanage, magnanimously allowed us to cook our own suppers in the tuck-room on Sunday evenings; the equipment and food being, of course, bought by ourselves out of our Pound a Term and Sixpence a Week fortunes. Woolworths, which really was the Sixpenny and Threepenny Store in those days, supplied all the gear—methylated spirit stove, frying-pan, tin plate, knife and fork. A pound of beef sausages (pork ones were too dear) a packet of beef dripping and a bag of spuds—between two of us. The tuck-room, decorated about ten years earlier on the lines of a local government outer office; tuck-boxes, in all stages of dilapidation, round the edge of the ancient wooden floor; coats, O.T.C. tunics and games clothes hanging round the walls, because there was nowhere else to keep them—the squalor would have been a disgrace to even a German prison-camp.

Our stove never seemed to give out as much heat as other people's—also we put far too much fat in the pan. We used to sit for what seemed hours watching those pink bangers floating around in amber-coloured, warm grease. The shiny new frying-pan seemed to resist all our efforts to hot it up. If you like burst, grease-sodden sausages (beef) and raw chips warmed through in beef dripping, you must let me give you the recipe sometime! The end came one winter's evening. Our supper was as near done as it was ever likely to be, when some clumsy lout caught his foot in the outfit, upsetting it on to a coconut mat beside the door into the "garden". The resulting blaze did disappointingly little damage. Had it burnt the House down, I would have felt more compensated for the loss of my supper.

VEAL

Veal, with the calf-raising policy as it is today, is somewhat of a rarity. So much so, that I suspiciously wonder whether the calf it came from wasn't a "bad-doer" to get knocked off at all! The reason that I have grouped pork and veal together is that they are the only white meats in general use, apart from poultry, of course. Their uses are very similar also—and often interchangeable. I am very sure few people, including myself, could spot the difference if they were given a Wiener Schnitzel made from pork instead of veal. The whole subject of the influence of the mind and the eye on not only the sense of taste but on the entire digestive system, is quite remarkable. One's stomach is very susceptible to propaganda—quite apart from the irritating trick of "playing up" at times of emotional stress, anxiety or apprehension.

A "family story" told to me by an old friend provides a good example of this. One of his ancestors was a sporting squire in the days when famous eccentrics were riding on bulls and using pigs trained as pointers, driving around the country with a four-in-hand of red deer instead of horses; and steeplechasing in their nightshirts. Bawdy, rumbustious times, when a gentleman hunted and shot all day; wenched and drank all night; eating, when time permitted, enormous meals to restore his strength for further sporting. This particular character was famous (or notorious?) in the county for his practical jokes. One day he shot a young vixen, and forthwith sent messages to some of his shooting and hunting friends, inviting them to come to dinner with him the following week to share the magnificent hare he had got.

History does not relate what he did to the fox to make it edible; salt and water for two days and a marinade of brandy and port for a week, I should think! But the fact remains that he and his chums ate the lot and agreed that it was the best hare they had ever eaten. Then he told them they had just eaten a fox. One by one, according to the time the news took to hit their tums with its full impact, they rushed out into the garden and heaved it up again. All except their diabolical host who, having eaten as much fox as anyone else, was laughing himself sick at their discomfiture.

The moral of this story (apropos of the pork or veal schnitzels) is—if whatever you are given to eat looks good, smells good, tastes good, and hasn't poisoned you, never enquire what it is made of! If you have a well-trained stomach, like the old squire, you can, of course, please yourself!

I think the reason for many people's dislike of veal is that they have had it under-cooked at some time. It then has a slimy texture, which is quite nauseating. Usually when it is roast it is first boned and then stuffed with forcemeat. Cook slowly for a long time, basting frequently to prevent drying, because veal has practically no fat on it.

Stewing veal is exactly the same as stewing pork. Flour and fry the meat and the chopped vegetables; cover with white wine, cider, beer or water and stew until tender. For myself, I consider it a dull flavourless meat, and would rather have a good rabbit any day.

* ❀ *

CHAPTER XI

OFFALS

OFFALS is the ugly-sounding word applied to all the edible parts of an animal apart from the dressed-out carcase itself. As many of these pieces weigh only a few ounces—compared with the half-ton of the live animal—it is not surprising that they are met with only rarely, or that the recipient has no idea how to prepare and cook them.

The first thing you must realise, when dealing with all the stuff in this section, is that it will never Let you Off—or even Let You Down Lightly. If offals are meticulously prepared and properly cooked, they are delicious. If they aren't, they are filthy. It's as easy as that. Sweetbreads not cleared of the fat and gristle adhering to them and undercooked—liver with pipes in it—brains that look like grey scrambled egg—oxtail only cooked for a couple of hours, and consequently like rubber—to mention but a few. I steer very clear of all offals in restaurants and hotels, unless I happen to know that the chef knows his job.

LIVER

Being the largest and probably the most popular of the offals, liver had better come first.

Calf's liver and lamb's liver (apparently it is still lamb's liver even if it has come out of a ten-year-old ram) are the ones used for frying—liver and bacon, etc. Pig's liver can be used for either, but—personal opinion only—is inferior to the other kinds, and better made into highly-seasoned pâtés. It is unlikely that you will get hold of any real calf liver these days, as so few calves are being slaughtered; and anyway, calves, like lambs, have the secret of eternal youth—according to the butchers! The state of health of an animal can usually be seen from the appearance of the liver; it should be of a darkish red colour, without pale patches, especially towards the thin end.

When cut, the texture should be uniform and not speckled. Refuse to buy liver with pipes in it—you can get dog-food far cheaper than that!

Cattle, and sometimes sheep, are prone to a disease called Liver-fluke. This parasite has a ridiculously complicated life-cycle, part of which is spent inside a water-snail which the cow eats along with a mouthful of grass in a damp water-meadow. The egg, or larval form, or whatever it is, then gets into the liver of its unwilling host, and grows into a leaf-shaped creature about half-an-inch long. It has a vague resemblance to a fluke or flounder, which gives it its name. It lives in the ducts, and turns the walls of them from an elastic tube into a thick calcified pipe. Sometimes it does so much damage that the host is killed, but usually the cow recovers, and seems to become reasonably immune to further attacks. The Ministry inspectors at the slaughter-houses are very particular indeed to see that none of this infected liver shall find its way to the public, but no one can be everywhere at once; and rogues abound, like fleas on a dog, so watch the liver being sliced before you buy it.

And so, if you are going to make liver-and-bacon, or cook it as part of a mixed grill, buy lamb's liver. Have it sliced between a quarter and half-an-inch thick. Fry it in lard, olive oil, pea-nut oil, or anything you like—but fry it slowly. The result to be aimed at is that the liver shall be cooked through, without the outside becoming hard. You can, if you like, dust the pieces with flour before frying but, as it will not be casseroled afterwards (and thus have gravy to be thickened) this is unnecessary. Put the liver in the pan and cook it until beads of blood appear on the upper side; turn it over and cook for the same length of time on the other side.

Ox liver should always be stewed, or casseroled, or it will be tough. Have it cut at least half-an-inch thick. To make the traditional liver-and-onions (which is hard to better) collect up three fair-sized onions and a pound of ox liver. Peel and slice the onions in half-inch rings. Dust them in flour, and fry until golden brown. Put them in a layer in a casserole, and then flour and fry the liver in the same way as lamb's liver. Put it on top of the onion, leaving as few spaces as possible, season with salt, black pepper and a large pinch of cayenne pepper. Flavour it with bay leaf, thyme, marjoram or rosemary, whichever you prefer. Cover with boiling water and simmer for at least two hours. It is practically impossible to overcook liver. Serve with creamed potato and any other vegetable you like. Carrots seem to go with it well.

KIDNEY

Kidney follows the same pattern as liver. Those used for frying come from the sheep, or sometimes the pig; and an ox kidney is always stewed. All kidney has a thin membrane covering it; this has, as a rule, been removed before you buy beef kidney. To prepare a sheep kidney, lay it on the table and, with a very sharp knife, cut it in half—the blade of the knife being parallel to the table. Now take hold of the edge of this membrane and peel it off each of the two halves. With the cut side uppermost, cut out the whitish core from both pieces. Fry slowly, so that the middle becomes well cooked without overdoing the outside. The method of dealing with a pig kidney, for frying, is exactly the same; but I suggest that stewing is the better way of cooking them. The flavour is otherwise inclined to be a bit rank.

Ox kidney has already been dealt with under Steak-and-Kidney pie, but again, briefly—cut it longitudinally down the middle and cut the edible part away from the white core. Slice into lumps about the size of the end joint of your thumb. In order to make one of the best breakfasts I know, flour and fry the kidney, put it in a casserole, season with salt, black pepper and cayenne pepper; cover with boiling water and simmer in the oven for at least three hours—or leave in a slow oven over-night. The resulting stew should be of a rich, dark colour, and the gravy should be fairly thick. Now, fry a half-inch slice of bread, on one side only, and a couple of rashers of bacon. Add a good dollop of kidney and whack in!

HEART

Both sheep and bullock hearts are usually roasted—or rather baked with dripping—in the oven.

SHEEP HEART

Cut away all the top part—fat, gristle, pipes, etc. and also the division between the compartments inside. Stuff with force-meat, cover with fat bacon, and roast for a couple of hours, basting frequently to prevent drying. Serve *very* hot.

OX HEART

This is probably at its best as Mock Goose and, if done properly, tastes and looks more like goose than the genuine article sometimes does! Remember the unlikely story of the chef who made a magnificent dish from a pair of lady's kid gloves? Others of the Brethren are equally expert at making goose taste like a lady's glove!

Cut away the top, and divisions, and simmer in salted water for three hours. Stuff with sage and onion, cover with fat bacon, and dot with lard. Wrap in cooking foil and roast for another one to two hours in a slow oven. It is not a good idea to attempt roasting for the whole cooking time, because it is impossible to prevent excessive drying-out. Serve with apple sauce. Any left-overs make quite good sandwiches.

SWEETBREADS

Sweetbreads are glands which are only found (in edible form anyway) in young animals. The thymus in the throat—which, in both sheep and cattle is rather the shape of a forked carrot, and another near the top of the heart. This one is squarish in shape, and the best from a culinary angle. I don't know what its function is.

Supposing that you have got the sweetbreads just as they were removed from the animal—with lumps of fat and gristle still adhering to them. Put them in a bowl and leave them under a cold running tap for at least an hour. This will get the remaining blood out. Now blanch them; to do this, place in a pan of cold salted water, and bring to the boil. Boil for five minutes and then take off the fire and allow to cool in the liquid. The actual preparation is easier whilst the sweetbreads are still warm. Your fingers are the only tools you need. Strip off all the fat, meat and gristle, and you will find, especially in the ox variety, that the gland itself is composed of a series of lobes, and is covered by a thin membranous skin. Take the lobes apart, removing at the same time as much of the skin as possible. There will be some small blood-vessels here and there. Take them out as well. You now have a pile of dissected sweet-bread, and a pile of rubbish. Take care that you throw the right one to the dogs, which will have been patiently drooling for the last quarter-of-an-hour. Once upon a time a friend of mine came home from a party in a somewhat hilarious state, went to the larder to get the fillet steak he had bought for his own supper, and the lump of shin for his Labrador's supper—need I go further? Anyone can make a mistake—as the hedge-hog said as he fell off the scrubbing-brush!

The other ingredients you will need for this dish are: an equal volume each of sliced onion and mushrooms (these either whole buttons or quartered larger ones), a pint of DRAUGHT cider—beer will do at a pinch but isn't so good—flour, herbs, and the usual peppers and salt.

Dust the onion in flour and fry it until it goes transparent, but not coloured. Put it in a casserole. Flour and fry the sweet-breads till they have just gone golden. Pack them, with the mushrooms, on top of the onion. Flavour and season, and then cover with cider. Cook gently for about an hour—or until light pressure with the edge of a fork against the side of the pot will cut a sweetbread in two.

The cooking of lamb sweetbreads is just the same. The difference is that they are easier to prepare and only take half the time in the oven.

LAMB'S FRY

Lamb's Fry is the trade name for young ram's testicles. Whether, if housewives knew what lamb's fry actually is, there would be a run on it, because of the sympathetic magic inevitably associated with it or whether it would be spurned as being rather rude, is anybody's guess. It is also sometimes sold as sweetbreads. The season for use is the Spring, when it is about the size and shape of a duck egg. Later on, in the Summer, the flavour becomes a bit rank.

The preparation is the same as for sweetbreads: Leave in running water for an hour or so; blanch and allow to cool. With a very sharp knife, cut through the two skins covering it; starting at the top, bring the knife down the side and rather past bottom centre. Peel both membranes off together. You now have a thing which looks like a large hard-boiled egg with a roughened surface. Starting at one end, cut it into half-inch slices.

Early in the season, probably the best way of cooking is to coat with egg and breadcrumb, and fry. Hence the name, I suppose. But later on I would advise cooking in cider—in the same way as lamb sweetbreads. The cooking time will be even shorter. Cooked by the first method, they should be served with fried bacon, mushrooms, and tomatoes, as a kind of mixed grill.

BRAINS

Brains are not easy to come by these days—ox brains, I am talking about. Sheep have such small brains that they are hardly worth bothering about—the reason for this is that nearly all cattle now are either naturally polled, or else are dehorned at some stage in their lives. The bullying, with its resulting injuries (sometimes severe), loss of condition, and loss of milk yield, which occurs in a herd of horned cows, makes this de-horning a very sensible practice. More bullocks can also be fed in a covered yard if they are polled. Horn was one of the saleable by-products of the slaughter-house, so the horns were axed off the skull with a cleaver. This left a hole through which the brains were easily extracted. Now that there are no horns to remove, it is not considered an economical proposition to bash, or saw through a great bone box in order to recover a few ounces of substance that most people can't cook anyway!

However, supposing you do happen to get some, the best way of cooking them is this: Leave them in cold running water for an hour and then pick off all the bloodstained membrane. This is a tedious job, but if you leave it until after blanching, it becomes almost impossible. Then blanch—as for sweetbreads— and when cool, put on a plate to drain and become quite cold. Meanwhile you have mixed a bowl of frying batter (page 143). Cut the brains into lumps the size of a walnut, dip them in the batter and deep-fry them—only a few at a time, so that the fat will not be put off the boil. If you make a mixture of vinegar and demerara sugar, boil it up, thicken a little with cornflour, and add a tablespoon or so of Cumberland sauce, you can pour it over the brains and produce a pleasant variation of Chinese sweet and sour pork.

OX TONGUE

This is very expensive if bought by the tin, and not either difficult or much trouble to make for yourself from a fresh tongue. The finished article is usually of a better flavour and quality too.

To prepare a tongue for pickling, take a sharp knife and cut away all the fat from the root, and from underneath. There is a U-shaped bone in the tongue root. Work around this with the knife and take it out with as little meat adhering to it as possible. Lay the tongue on the table and, with a carving fork, prod holes deep into it all the way round, especially at the thick end. The purpose of this is to allow the pickle to penetrate more easily.

The pickle itself is simply a saturated solution of salt in cold water, with a teaspoonful of saltpetre and, if you like, some demerara sugar added. Mix this up in an earthenware container (or glass, or wood) leaving undissolved salt in the bottom. Immerse the tongue in the pickle for at least five days and at most a week.

Remove from the pickle, wash under the cold tap, place in a large pan of cold water, bring to the boil and boil gently for four hours. At the end of this time, allow the tongue to cool in the cooking liquor (which, by the way, will be so salt that it is practically useless as a base for soup, etc.) until you can handle it without burning yourself. Take it out and put it on a large meat dish—to give yourself room to manoeuvre—slit the skin from the base to the tip, straight up the middle, and carefully peel it off. Cut away any other bits you don't like the look of. You probably do not have a tongue-press—neither do I—but a perfectly efficient substitute is easily rigged up. My own tongue-pressing gear consists of a 2½-pint, straight-sided saucepan which I curl the tongue into; a 3-lb. stone jam-pot, which is a fair fit in the pan and is placed, bottom down, on top of the tongue. The last piece of equipment is a very heavy crowbar, which must weigh upwards of 60-lbs. Whilst still as warm as possible, the tongue is put in the pan, and a very little cooking liquor poured in to moisten. The pan is then placed on the floor in the angle between the wall and a cupboard. The jar is stood on top, and the crowbar stood in the jar and propped in the angle to prevent it falling. Leave overnight and then pour some hot water over the pan, to melt the tongue loose, and gently pull it out—still stuck firmly to the bottom of the jar. Cut away and put on a plate. The result looks most professional.

OX TAIL

If properly cooked, ox-tail is as good a meal as you could wish for on a cold winter's day. If the tail is very fresh, hang it for two or three days in summer, or a week in winter. This will not only improve the flavour but also the texture. Cutting an ox-tail into its separate vertebrae requires a little experience. If you lay the tail on the table with the top side uppermost, you will notice a line of narrow, oval, yellowish bumps running down the centre and, of course, becoming smaller towards the thin end. These bumps are a useful guide to the location of the joint. As far as I remember, the place to cut is about three-quarters way down these marks—starting from the top end. Anyway, take the tail off its hook and trim off all the fat you possibly can. Cut into separate vertebrae as far down as is sensible: the last four or five inches is useless to eat but can be put in the pot to help the gravy.

Peel and slice four medium-sized onions; flour them and fry

till they start to turn golden. Put into a casserole or into a heavy iron pot, if you have not got an oven. You will have noticed that, whenever possible, I recommend you to cook stews in the oven, rather than in a pot on the fire or stove. There are two reasons for this. First, and more important, the food does not stick to the pan and burn—especially if the oven has a top heat—because the cooking is done by hot air, or convection, and not radiation or direct heat. Secondly, as the heat is comparatively steady in an oven, it can be set to a pitch where the food will cook without boiling dry.

Flour and fry the sections of tail. Whilst they are cooking, slice up a few carrots and put them on the onions. When the tail is browned, pack the pieces into the onion and season with cayenne, black pepper, and salt; add a sprinkle of mixed herbs. Cover with boiling water and simmer for not less than five hours—preferably six.

MARROW BONES

Marrow bones are made from the femur, or thigh-bone, of an ox. Saw the bones into two to three inch lengths, discarding the knuckles at either end. Seal the cut ends of the pieces with flour and water paste; wrap all the pieces up in a floured cloth, and boil for two hours. Marrow bones are boiled, and not roasted, because the higher temperature of the oven would cause the marrow to melt and run away. Remove the seals, and serve with dry toast. Alternatively, you can scoop the marrow out yourself, season it, and spread it on toast before you serve it. Reheat under the grill and serve as hot as possible.

HEAD

Sheep's head I have dealt with elsewhere; you *can* make sheep's head pie, and sheep's head broth if you wish, but I don't think you will enjoy eating either—and they are both a lot of trouble, the head having to be soaked in salt water, blanched, reboiled, etc. etc. For puppies, for which this palaver is not necessary, Yes—for humans, No.

Calf's head, in the last century, was evidently a very popular dish. I may have been unlucky, but the few times I have eaten it the texture was gelatinous to the point of sliminess. I didn't like it at all. Therefore I do not consider it would be honest were I to filch a recipe from elsewhere and put it in here. I have never cooked it, have no intention of trying, and wouldn't eat it anyway; and so, if you are interested, I commend you to Mrs. Beeton.

Pig's head, and Pig's trotters, are worth having for the meat that can be taken off them, the excellent stock they yield when boiled to destruction in a pressure-cooker, and a certain amount of lard that can be taken off the top when the stock cools. Half a head will probably be enough for you. Remove the eye and brains, and scrape off any hair still on it. Take off the end of the snout. Soak in salt water for twenty-four hours, and then blanch. Put in fresh water and boil for a couple of hours. Despumate—or skim—to begin with, to get rid of the rubbish which will rise to the top. Take out of the pot and allow to cool until you can take the meat off without getting burned. Put this on one side to use for Chinese dishes, curries, casseroles, etc. and put all the rest of the head—bones and all—into the pressure-cooker, and let it sizzle away until the bones begin to dissolve. Strain the stock off into a basin and throw the rest away. The hens might enjoy it perhaps, but they wouldn't get much nourishment out of it.

Trotters are dealt with in exactly the same way, and are particularly useful as a basis for soups in the winter—a sort of pork Scotch broth!

The other "pig products"—sausages, black pud., brawn, haislet, chitterlings, and Heaven knows what else—are all made professionally by the pork butchers and delicatessen merchants. (Who was it who said during the war, "A nation who would call *blut worst*—blood sausage—'delicatessen', *deserves* to be blasted out of existence"?) And so, if you like them, buy them —at least you haven't all the trouble of making them yourself.

PART FIVE

Cabbages & Kings

❁

CHAPTER XII

CABBAGES & KINGS

INEVITABLY, having sorted one's material as far as possible into chapters dealing with various aspects of the subject, one is left, at the end, with a heterogeneous collection of odds and ends which, although not seeming to fit in anywhere, might nevertheless prove useful.

BACON AND EGGS

Bacon and Eggs is possibly the only breakfast—or only meal, come to that—which most people can eat every day for years on end, without becoming sick of the sight of it. I discovered also that it was the only meal that I could eat before taking off on a bombing raid over Germany, without getting violent indigestion during the flight. A cramped position over the controls, coupled with a fairly high degree of nervous tension, made a stodgy supper quite impossible.

Now, you know as well as I do the difference between coming down in the morning and being presented with a hot plate containing a couple of compact, white, fried eggs; bacon which is crinkly, almost crisp, and a clear red and cream colour; tomatoes that are cooked, but still retain their shape; and finally a slice of fried bread that is a light golden colour, crisp yet soft, and fried on one side only—there being no visible sign of fat on either the food or the plate: and the antithesis—a lukewarm plate from which two boot-soled eggs glare up at your with baleful orange eyes (pale primrose, if they are battery eggs!), strips of brownish substance, black-speckled, and with the texture of inner tube; sorrowful soppy little heaps of reddish stuff, perhaps burnt a little black in places; and a slab of bread, the crusts still on it, either grey and grease-sodden, or else black round the edges and still white in the middle. Not a good start to the day, but unfortunately the latter technique has become the norm, and the former something to be wondered at.

The first thing to realise is that cooking bacon and eggs is a full-time job. You cannot, at the same time, make the coffee or toast; neither can you nip down to feed the hens. If you are cooking on a gas ring, your work will be very much easier because the heat is instant and infinitely variable. Also heat follows the bottom of the pan, whatever angle it may be.

Use a thick-bottomed pan, preferably aluminium; heat it, and then polish it out with a crumpled piece of newspaper till it is completely clean. Replace on the stove and put in a lump of lard. When choosing your bacon, go for the roll or flitch which has quite a large quantity of fat on it—and the fat with rather a pinkish tinge about it. Have it cut one or two notches thinner than the usual thickness, then it will crinkle in the pan and look more attractive—and you can afford an extra slice all round! Cut the rind off it, and cut the rashers in two. When you can see the faintest, almost invisible vapour coming off the frying pan, the fat is boiling. Put in the bacon and fry it until the fat on it goes transparent; then turn it over and continue cooking till the fat goes opaque again. Remove and put in a warm oven.

Take the pan off the stove for a few minutes to allow the fat to go off the boil. Eggs should be cooked in hot but not boiling, fat. Turn down the gas and replace the pan with the far edge over the flame. Tip it away from you so that there is a small pond of fat in the angle. Prop the pan in this position with a piece of coal or a fragment of that cup you've just dropped, and break two eggs into the fat, side by side. You can baste them either by flicking fat over them with the tip of the spatula, or by ladling it with a spoon—the idea being to cook the egg from both top and bottom at the same time, thereby avoiding a gelatinous top and a leathery bottom. When an air bubble comes up over the yolk, take the egg out at once. It is cooked.

FRIED BREAD

Cut the slices half-an-inch thick and trim off the crusts; if this is not done, the crust forms a rim which gets burned, and at the same time lifts the centre of the slice clear of the pan, thereby preventing it from cooking. Bring the fat up to the boil again, put the bread in and, if necessary, hold the centre of the slice down on to the pan with the spatula to ensure even cooking. Remove when pale golden brown. Fry on one side only.

TOMATOES

These are better cooked in another frying pan, on their own. Cut them in half, crossways, and put in the pan cut side uppermost. Cook slowly for about a quarter of an hour; sprinkle with a little salt, and a grind of black pepper. The half tomatoes are not fried so much as boiled in their skins —greasiness thereby being impossible.

MUSHROOMS

Mushrooms can be eaten raw and so do not need much cooking. They diminish in size very rapidly, and your nice big mushroom will be no bigger than a trouser button if you don't watch it! Fry them in butter—gill side down for half a minute, and then three to four minutes on the domed side. Butter is tricky stuff to fry with. Hardly has the water boiled out of it before it begins to go brown, and burn. So turn the heat down as soon as the mushrooms are sizzling and then, when they are cooked, pour the remaining scrap of butter over them—but not too much.

CREAMED MUSHROOMS

Put a pound of button mushrooms, two ounces of butter, and the juice of half a lemon, in a heavy saucepan. Season and simmer, with the lid on, for about half an hour. Meanwhile mix a dessertspoon of flour with a quarter pint of milk, so that it forms a smooth cream. Add this to the mushrooms, bring to the boil, and simmer for a further ten minutes to cook the flour. Serve with bacon and fried bread.

EGGS

It is rather odd that the egg should be held up as an example at both ends of the culinary competence scale. "Huh, she she can't even boil an egg." Yet no less an authority than Escoffier himself (bow, please!) says that the correct scrambling of eggs denotes a high degree of efficiency on the part of the cook.

BOILED:

For a medium/large egg: place in boiling water for four-and-a-half minutes. The white will then be completely set, and the yolk still liquid.

FRIED:

See Bacon and Eggs.

POACHED:

Break the eggs into a pan of salted boiling water with a dash of vinegar added. Reduce heat immediately so that the water is just moving. Cook for three minutes, and then remove from the water with a slotted draining-spoon. The white will have wrapped itself round the yolk, re-forming itself into an eggshape. Serve on buttered toast.

SCRAMBLED

Melt a lump of butter in a small saucepan. Meanwhile lightly beat the eggs, adding half a shell of water for each two eggs, salt and black pepper. Pour into the pan and stir continuously over a low heat. When the eggs start to thicken, take the pan off and add more butter—cut off in thin slices so that it will melt quickly. Continue stirring till the butter has disappeared, and the accumulated heat in the metal of the pan has thickened the eggs to the correct consistency. Naturally, the heavier the pan, the earlier it can be taken off the heat. The point of adding most of the butter right at the end is that it retains its flavour of fresh butter which, if it were cooked with the egg, it would not.

OMELETTE

This is really just a lazy way of making scrambled eggs! Put a very small piece of butter in a clean frying-pan—just enough to prevent the contents sticking. Use two to three eggs for each omelette, and beat them up in a basin. If you want to make a fluffy omelette, give the eggs a good working-over with a wind-up egg beater, immediately before pouring into the pan. When the pan is hot, tip the beaten egg gently in. Reduce heat, otherwise the bottom of the omelette will become brown and it will taste predominantly of burnt butter instead of egg. As soon as it has set enough, lift the edge with a spatula and allow some of the unset part from the top to run underneath. Do this at intervals round the pan. Whilst there is still some liquid left on top, put in your filling of kidney, mushrooms, etc.—already cooked, of course—and fold in half. Slide out on to a hot plate and serve immediately.

BATTER

Knowing nothing, first hand, about batter, I cannot do better than filch a recipe straight out of Mrs. Beeton's Household Management for you.

"Coating Batter. (1).
2 ozs. Plain flour.
Pinch of salt.
1 dessertspn salad oil or oiled
  butter.

$\frac{1}{2}$ gill warm water.
1 egg white.

Sift together the flour and the salt. Mix to a smooth consistency with the oil and water. Beat well and leave to stand for at least 30 min. Just before using, stiffly whisk the egg white and then stir it lightly into the batter."

Whilst we are about it, you may as well have the recipe for pancakes and for Yorkshire pudding. The method of making the batter is identical for both, and is given in "Mrs. Beeton" as—

Basic Recipe

BATTER PUDDING

½ lb. plain flour.	1 pint milk.
¼ teasp salt.	1 tablespn cooking fat, or lard.
2 eggs.	

Sift the flour and salt into a basin. Make a well in the centre of the flour and break the eggs into this. Add about a gill of the milk. Stir gradually working the flour down from the sides and adding more milk, as required, to make a stiff batter consistency. Beat well for about 5 min. Add the rest of the milk. Cover and leave to stand for thirty minutes. Put the fat into a Yorkshire pudding tin and heat in the oven until hot. The fat should just be beginning to smoke. Quickly pour in the batter and leave to cook in a hot oven (425F or Gas 7.) at the top of the oven until nicely browned. Reduce the heat to 375F, Gas 5. and finish cooking through for 10-15 mins.

Serve with wine—, syrup—, or jam sauce.

6 helpings.

Time.	(Large pudding)	—35-40 mins.
	(Individual puddings)	—20-25 mins."

Flossie who, by odd coincidence, happens to be around—and looking over my shoulder—says, "Put a couple more eggs in—it will be much nicer." But Flossie, as you may have gathered, is inclined to impulsive generosity; so I leave it to you whether you take her advice or not!

CORN FRITTERS

Corn Fritters are sometimes a useful variation on the pan-cake theme. Use instead of potato with such dishes as fried chicken, grills, bacon and eggs etc. Make about half a pint of pan-cake batter, and then, having first strained off the liquid, tip in a can of sweet corn—the kind with separate grains, taken off the cob. Libbys make a very good one. Stir up well, and drop, in spoonfuls, into a lightly greased frying pan. Cook on both sides, and serve hot.

VENISON

This is a meat which has been held in very high esteem since the earliest times—and with good reason. But, along with hare and pigeon, which in many ways it resembles, it seems to have fallen into disrepute since the Kaiser's War. Sometimes it cannot be sold at all, at others it fetches sixpence a pound as dog's meat. This is merely another example of the ignorance and idleness so prevalent in the supermarket era.

A deer usually browses when it feeds; that is, he nibbles leaves and shoots from trees, shrubs and plants—and bark, too, in winter when there is little else. This probably accounts for the different flavour venison has from meat off a grazing animal, such as a sheep or cow.

The Roe Deer (the only one of which I have first-hand experience) is one of the most graceful and beautiful of all British wild animals; and so, if you ever shoot a covert where roe are being driven past the guns, extend to them the courtesy that is their right. Personally, I am always stricken with a strange paralysis of the arms which makes the lifting of my gun quite impossible (and, incidentally, earned me some black looks from my host). But if you must shoot them, never fire at more than ten yards if your gun is loaded with a game charge (shot sizes from 7 to 4), and even if you are using special cartridges loaded with buck-shot, don't fire at over twenty yards. Go for a heart shot—behind the shoulder—and if you have any doubt about killing, don't fire at all. There are few things that cast a worse blight on a shooting party than seeing a wounded deer get away. Anyway, in my opinion, they should always be shot with a rifle.

However, we will suppose that, on this occasion, a deer has been shot. It should be gralloched straight away—this is exactly the same process as paunching a rabbit. Open up the abdomen, and remove the stomach and intestines. Take the carcase to the nearest point where it can be picked up by transport, and hang it up by the hind legs. When you get it home, slit the diaphragm and take out the lungs, heart, and liver. The latter is a great delicacy, and should be eaten as soon as possible. Cut in slices, between a quarter and half-an-inch thick, and fry with bacon. The Scottish stalker has the Red-deer liver as his traditional "perk", after the laird, or one of his guests, has completed a successful stalk.

If you have a large, airy larder, hang the deer up in it. If you haven't, find someone else who has. Beware of bluebottles, if it is that time of year. The longer venison hangs—within reason, of course—the tenderer it will be, and the better the flavour. As a very rough guide, give it a fortnight if the temperature is around 40° F., a week if around 50° F., and only three days at 60° F. and over. Dress the carcase out in exactly the same manner as is given in the chapter on mutton for dressing a sheep. The cutting into joints is similar, but I would recommend you to cut the shoulders away from the rib-cage, and then chop the latter up into pieces that will go into the pressure cooker, and reduce it to stock, with five or six hours' boiling. Don't try to saw the loin into two sets of chops—it isn't big enough. And, finally, don't make the mistake that I did once—of cutting off the hind feet too high up, so that I cut the Achilles tendons, and had nothing to hang it up by.

Now for the cooking. Except in very isolated instances, when the venison has a reasonable quantity of fat on it (and there is very seldom much fat on any wild animals) I do not recommend roasting. As with hare, the meat is too dry, and you will be taking a quite unnecessary risk of wasting your joint.

Having asked Lettie to supper, and got her wide-eyed with

admiration at the story of yourself, in the role of the intrepid White Hunter fearlessly facing the charge of a maddened stag, simply in order that she shall dine on venison, you don't want to give her a slice of stringy old stuff she can't get her teeth into, do you? The fact that you bought it for a couple of pints from a local poaching layabout you met in the pub need never come to light!

You have a haunch, or hind leg. With a very sharp knife, cut the meat away from the bone, and put the latter in the pressure cooker to make stock. There is a thin membranous skin covering the meat—the same as that on shin beef, only not so tough. Cut and pull this off. Dissect the meat roughly into its separate muscles, and leave it in lumps four or five inches long, and two or three thick. Trim up so that the pieces look attractive, and have no rubbish on them. Peel a medium-sized onion and slice it very finely. Pack a layer of meat into a big glass, or earthenware bowl, and scatter some onion, pepper and salt on top. Repeat until the meat is used up, then pour in red wine until it is covered. Draught cider will do, but I prefer wine for this purpose. Leave in this marinade for twenty-four hours.

At the end of this time, take the pieces out and dry them. Flour them, then fry in butter or olive oil (or a mixture of both, if you like) till the flour has turned light brown. Put them in a casserole, add a little cayenne, some black pepper, a sprinkling of mixed herbs, and salt. There will be a little butter, and some brown sediment of flour remaining in the frying pan. Scatter enough flour into the butter to "take it up" in the form of a *roux*. Cook for a few minutes, and then pour in the marinade—onions and all—or, as the professionals say, "Swill the pan". Let this bubble away until a thick, smooth gravy has formed, then pour it through a strainer, into the casserole. Top up with the stock from the pressure-cooked rib-cage and/or bones, and simmer for a couple of hours, or until tender. Now pour the cooking liquor off into a heavy saucepan, add a dessertspoon of red-currant jelly, and simmer till this has melted. Take off the fire, allow to cool for five minutes, then stir in at least one glass of drinkable port.

Pour back over the venison, after you have tasted it and adjusted the salt and flavourings—if necessary.

You may do all this hours (or even the day) before you want to use it. All you need do is to put it in a medium oven for half-an-hour to get hot, but not to boil again. Serve with creamed potato, and the best fresh vegetables available at the time.

SCALLOPS

A bivalve which seems to have two main varieties. First, the true scallop which has one shell flat, and shaped like a fan; and the other very curved, to form a small dish. They are quite large, some measuring upwards of five inches across. The other kind are called "Queens" in some parts of the country; these are only about three inches in diameter, and both shells are curved.

The edible part of both consists of the column of white muscle which opens and closes the shell, and a small yellow or orange piece which looks rather like a segment from a tangerine. This has a black bit at the end of it which should be removed by pinching it out between the thumb nail and the first finger.

To prepare scallops, I use a screwdriver and a table knife which has been sharpened round the end. Push the screwdriver into the little gap near the hinge of the shell, and twist it enough to be able to slide the knife down the flat shell, cutting the muscle free. Open the scallop, and cut the column of muscle loose from the curved shell by sliding the knife end under it. You now have a nasty, frilly, slimy-looking mess in the shell. Sort out the white muscle and the orange segment, take the black piece off, and put them on a separate plate. Throw all the rest away. Queens are prepared in exactly the same way, but are more fiddling because you need more of them to produce the same result. When you have done the lot, wash them again to make sure no sand remains. If prepared scallops are left in cold water overnight, they will swell considerably. This is what has been done with those unbelievably large dressed scallops you sometimes see on-fishmongers' slabs.

There are three main ways of cooking them and the method you choose depends first, of course, on which you like best, and then on how many people you have to feed on the quantity of scallops available. If the dredges have hit a lucky drift and the market is knee-deep, the price will fall very low. Shortly after the war I sometimes used to buy them on the waterfront at Brixham for a penny each. But this doesn't happen very often—luckily for the fishermen. However, supposing this to have been the case and extravagance is no object, simply fry them in butter and serve with bacon and fried bread. I will be surprised if, however hungry you are, you can get through more than a dozen—they are quite remarkably bodging. Alternatively:

SCALLOPS IN WHITE SAUCE

Clean a third as many curved shells as you have scallops, butter them well and scatter with breadcrumbs. Put three scallops in each, season with salt and cayenne, scatter in some chopped parsley, and add a squeeze of lemon juice. Fill the shells up with thick white sauce and put some more bread-crumbs on top. Dot with butter and bake in the oven for ten to fifteen minutes.

SCALLOPED SCALLOPS

Scalloped scallops is the last stage before you decide you really haven't enough, and keep those you have got, for your own breakfast tomorrow! It is exactly the same as the previous recipe, except that the scallops are finely chopped, and mixed with the same volume of breadcrumbs. Add the same seasoning and flavouring and bind the mixture together with white sauce. Put it in the buttered shells; more crumbs and lumps of butter on top. Bake till browned.

MUSSELS

Mussels always taste best when you have gathered them yourself, picking out the biggest and best, from the mussel-beds at low tide. Check up, locally, that there is no pollution that affects the beds, because a contaminated mussel is exceedingly poisonous.

The most tedious part of a mussel dish comes first. Using a blunt old kitchen knife, you must scrape the shells clean of all barnacles, mud and weed; then scrub them with a brush and rinse in several waters. This is quite something when you reckon at least a pint of mussels per head! Whilst you are doing this chore, twist the shells of each one, to check that they are alive, and of course, discard any which are open or cracked.

MOULES MARINIÈRE

Moules Marinière is probably the best way of cooking them —furthermore it sounds rather ritzier than Mussel Stoo!

Collect up:

Fifty mussels.	Half pint of dry white wine.
Four or five shallots. (or one equivalent onion).	Three tablespoons chopped parsley.
Butter.	Thyme.
	Bay leaf.
Black pepper mill.	

Fry the shallots in butter (using a saucepan large enough to hold the mussels) until they are soft, but not browned. Add the wine and the herbs. Grind in some pepper. Simmer this concoction for about a quarter of an hour, and then tip the cleaned mussels in. Cover and continue cooking—shaking the pan all the time—until the shells open. Strain the liquor off into another pan, and allow it to be reducing whilst you are taking the mussels out of the shells and putting them in a suitably-sized dish. Now make a *roux* in yet another pan, by melting a lump of butter about an inch cube, and scattering enough flour into it to form a soft paste. Add the cooking liquor gradually to the *roux,* stirring hard to avoid lumpiness. When at the correct consistency, allow to cook for ten minutes (still stirring) and then pour over the mussels.

Alternatively, you can coat the mussels with egg and bread-crumbs when they are taken out of the shells, and fry them. The sauce is made in the same way, but is served separately.

VEGETABLES

Far too many vegetables are spoiled in the cooking—and nearly always because they have been *over*-cooked. New potatoes that are crumbling to pieces; pinkish-yellow Brussels sprouts, mushy, and with a horrible flavour; that unspeakable boiled cabbage which everyone has had the misfortune to encounter at some time or another. All these are due to nothing else than too long cooking. Apart from the appearance and taste, the dieticians say that most of the vitamins are ruined as well. And so, as there is no point in my trying to tell you how to prepare and cook all the various things in this book, and then let you spoil your efforts with soggy vegetables, I had better include a little basic vegetable cooking.

POTATOES

Pommes Naturel (in other words, plain boiled spuds): Use old potatoes. Peel them, take out the "eyes" and wire-worm holes, and cut them in half—partly to make them cook faster, and partly to see that they are not rotten in the middle. Put them in cold water, add some salt, and bring to the boil. Continue boiling for about thirty-five minutes, or until a fork can easily be stuck into them. Drain, and serve.

CREAMED POTATOES

Cook the potatoes exactly as in the preceding paragraph and then, after draining, mash them. Add slices of butter (for quicker melting) black pepper, and more salt if necessary.

When the butter has melted, stir well and at intervals add a little milk. When you reach a consistency at which it is possible to do so, beat it into a thick, creamy, smooth paste. A very little finely-chopped raw onion sprinkled in before the final beating, is quite a good idea, with some dishes.

NEW POTATOES

New Potatoes are at their best when scrubbed and boiled as soon as they have been dug out of your own potato patch; and so do not either dig up, or buy, more than you need for immediate use. When straight out of the ground, they only need a light scrub with a nail-brush; but after a day or two, will be better scraped to remove the skin. Place in cold water, bring to the boil, and cook for about a quarter of an hour. I find that the best way to get them right is to prod them with a fork every couple of minutes from ten onwards. As soon as the fork begins to penetrate, tip the water off and put a lump of butter and a sprig of mint in the pan. Shake up, and put in a warm (not hot) place till needed. The accumulated heat in the pan, and the potatoes themselves, will finish the cooking —and the smell of the mint, when you take the pan-lid off, makes the whole operation worthwhile.

CABBAGE

Cabbage is not my favourite vegetable, but I have found a method of preparing and cooking which renders it quite eatable. Cut a hard, white cabbage into quarters, lengthways, and then, with a large, razor-sharp knife, slice it across as finely as you can. Aim at the thickness of navy-cut tobacco. Cut away the solid stalks. Don't be dismayed by the seemingly enormous volume of sauerkrautish looking stuff you have produced. Put it into a saucepan, add salt, pour boiling water on it till it is almost covered, bring to the boil again and cook for THREE MINUTES. Strain very thoroughly—preferably in a large sieve—and add plenty of butter and a generous grinding of black pepper. Mix up well, and serve. Alternatively you can pour white sauce over it instead of the butter.

BRUSSELS SPROUTS

Brussels Sprouts are probably the best of all the winter vegetables—provided, of course, that they are good, hard sprouts to begin with, and that the right person cooks them. Use a very sharp knife to prepare them. Slice off enough of the stem to free the two outer leaves, and peel them away. If the sprout still looks scruffy, take off another pair of leaves. Cut a cross in the solid end of the stem so that it will cook faster, and not be hard and woody when the rest is done. Leave in salt water for a quarter of an hour, to duff up any slugs, greenfly, or other wuggins you may have missed during preparation. Drain this water off and cover with boiling water, add salt, bring back to the boil and cook for SEVEN MINUTES. Drain, and butter and pepper. The sprouts will be of a good green colour; cooked, but with a very slight crispiness. The flavour should be excellent.

No matter what other vegetables you may cook—runner beans, cauliflower, carrot, artichoke, peas, broad beans, parsnips, beetroot—whether young or old: take them off the fire as soon as you can stick a fork into them, or can eat a piece you have fished out of the pan. Any further cooking is just gradual destruction.

And so we come to the end. I can take you no further, but if I have achieved my object of telling you, not what to make, or what to put in it, but HOW to make it—starting from first principles—then I am happy. If you want to go further, you must do the same as I and consult The Masters. I must leave you. The old compulsive urge for a bit of steak-and-kidney pie is stealing over me again. My weak will is one of my most prized possessions. Where's that telephone—

"Flossie, darling . . ."

THE END

INDEX

✿